W9-CAY-787

The Gift of Addiction

Sherry Burditt, RN, HN-BC

Balboa Press books may be ordered through booksellers or by contacting:

This book is a work of non-fiction. Unless otherwise noted, the author and the publisher make no explicit guarantees as to the accuracy of the information contained in this book and in some cases, names of people and places have been altered to protect their privacy.

The information, ideas, and suggestions in this book are not intended as a substitute for professional medical advice. Before following any suggestions contained in this book, you should consult your personal physician. Neither the author nor the publisher shall be liable or responsible for any loss or damage allegedly arising as a consequence of your use or application of any information or suggestions in this book.

Balboa Press
A Division of Hay House
1663 Liberty Drive
Bloomington, IN 47403
www.balboapress.com
1 (877) 407-4847

Because of the dynamic nature of the Internet, any web addresses or links contained in this book may have changed since publication and may no longer be valid. The views expressed in this work are solely those of the author and do not necessarily reflect the views of the publisher, and the publisher hereby disclaims any responsibility for them.

The author of this book does not dispense medical advice or prescribe the use of any technique as a form of treatment for physical, emotional, or medical problems without the advice of a physician, either directly or indirectly. The intent of the author is only to offer information of a general nature to help you in your quest for emotional and spiritual well-being. In the event you use any of the information in this book for yourself, which is your constitutional right, the author and the publisher assume no responsibility for your actions.

Print information available on the last page.

ISBN: 978-1-9822-0774-8 (sc)
ISBN: 978-1-9822-0775-5 (e)

Library of Congress Control Number: 2018908089

Balboa Press rev. date: 10/04/2018

To Toby, my heart and joy:

By your love and courage, this book has become a reality.
Thank you for helping me find the words.
I will love you eternally.

To my Family:

My husband Charles, who knows the joy and the pain;
and whose love, wisdom and devotion
bring me comfort and peace every day.

My beautiful daughters, Samahna and Meghann,
whose love, wisdom and huge hearts
bring me joy beyond description.

My littlest Peejie, who brings so much sunshine
into my heart, I think it will burst.

My sweet Jessica, Zachary, Henry, and Grady,
whose light and laughter fill my soul.

My mother Priscilla, my father James,
my brother Jamie, and my sisters Jody and Gardie,
I love you all more than you will ever know.

To all my Staff and Patients:

You have taught me everything I know
about the Gift of Addiction.

To my Spiritual Teacher, Paramahansa Yogananda:

My greatest devotion and gratitude to you
for your love, care, endless patience,

and faith in me.

A C K N O W L E D G E M E N T S

I acknowledge all the special souls who have supported the creation of this book:

♥

To all the addicts, alcoholics and their families who I have had the honor to work with, you never cease to amaze me with your love, wisdom and endless courage.

To Steve, my friend, mentor, and comrade – I treasure our 15 year partnership in the treatment of addiction. Your enduring faith and determination along the path have made this book possible.

To those of you who courageously shared your stories, thank you from the bottom of my heart for who you are, and all you give every day.

To Marty, without your determination, commitment, tenacity, and technical skills, this book would never have been written. Thank you doesn't express my gratitude.

To Stephanie, Melinda, and Jonna, thank you for your boundless energy, keeping me on track, and sending me home when necessary!!

To Caroline Myss, PhD, whose vast insight into Energy Medicine and the Chakras has given me and our patients a new understanding and appreciation for the "Gift of Addiction". Thank you so much for your priceless contribution.

To Barbara, my special friend and manuscript consultant – you walked this journey with me, having endless patience with my efforts to put thoughts into words. Thank you so much.

To Patty, Rose, Phil, Wendy, Jerry, Margaret, Shirley, Eileen, Tina, George, and Midgie, thank you all for your support and divine friendship…,always.

Thank you all ♥

FOREWORD

At first glance, the title of this book seems to disrespect the tragedy of addiction as we know it. The title might be the very reason you picked up this book in the first place. It is dumbfounding, counter intuitive, and even maddening, but it is also intriguing. After all, we, in this day and age, are facing the most overwhelming explosion of addiction issues ever to hit this country. Articles, news stories, popular media, and most content experts all describe addiction in the context of an epidemic. Merriam Webster defines an epidemic as, "affecting or tending to affect a disproportionately large number of individuals within a population, community, or region at the same time. Obviously, epidemic is not a word to use lightly. It is serious stuff. I could also venture to believe through your interest in this book, that you have been affected by addiction in some way; either personally, through an associate, or loved one, or hearing how the wrecking ball of addiction devastated an entire extended family. Many stories don't end well. Loss of health, position, self-respect, incarceration and even death are common place. For many, the sense of helplessness, hopelessness, and despair are overwhelming. This could be the end of the story. But wait, what about "The Gift of Addiction"? What could this mean? Is there a way out? The answers lay ahead.

I first met Sherry Burditt years ago, brought together quite randomly by a mutual associate, to work at a Psychiatric Hospital. She was brought in to be the facilities Director of Nursing, and I was brought in to establish a hospital based chemical dependency treatment service, something by that time I had become very proficient at doing. Shortly after we arrived, in a type of business coup usually reserved for much greater enterprises, our mutual associate was gone and new faces began to appear to replace him. For the next several months, Sherry and I met frequently to share information and provide mutual support as our current roles appeared less and less stable. I was impressed with the resilience and calm demeanor that Sherry consistently displayed during this entire period in which our foundations were shaken. Both of us ultimately moved on but from that day forward our personal and professional relationship was established.

Sherry went on a pilgrimage to India, started her own private practice, and became a Certified Holistic Nurse among other endeavors, and I went on to open another treatment center in Hemet, California. Shortly after opening, Sherry began working on the new unit, first as a consultant and ultimately as the Director of Clinical Services. We both possess mutually exclusive skill sets, and as such, became a very effective leadership team. Sherry's focus and commitment to personally provide clinical services to patients has never wavered. Her groups and sessions are consistently identified by patients as being the most helpful, life changing, and effective experiences they had while in treatment. Patients returning for alumni groups share their stories of continued success and growth over time.

I would describe Sherry's individual work with patients, in the context of our treatment program, as phenomenal. The most difficult and challenging cases are often reserved for Sherry. The positive results I have seen speak for themselves. In my mind, her credibility and the credibility of her approach are without question.

The current addiction epidemic and the front page attention it has created has placed a spotlight on the problem, and in turn, has created a cottage industry of solutions and remedies. Some approaches are main stream evidenced based and others are not. Everything from different forms of Intravenous Therapies, Brain Mapping, and Neurofeedback, to Medication Assisted Treatment and Epi- pens are offered as answers, or at least new tools for the recovery tool box. Most of this activity is positive, but is it the answer? The "Gift of Addiction" acknowledges life's bottom, so efficiently created by addiction, as the beginning. It is the opening of the door that allows for unimaginable opportunity. The many personal stories and anecdotes that are provided throughout the book create a personal connection to the approach to recovery being introduced. Along the way Sherry helps the reader identify "Gifts" that would ordinarily be overlooked or not acknowledged. These "Gifts" become understood as acts of love and are encouragement for the journey. The recovery that is possible, as suggested in this book, is authentic, honest, and filled with positive energy. It is time for you to understand the "Gift of Addiction".

Steven Collier, RN
Chief Executive Officer
Addiction Medicine Services, Inc.
Hemet Valley Recovery Center & Sage Retreat

TABLE OF CONTENTS

Chapter 1

The Gift of Addiction

Introduction

I know there is a reason you picked up this book. I also know that if you read it carefully, your life will change forever. It has been a very difficult book to write – to find the right words to explain the purpose for the suffering. But, it is my sincerest hope and prayer that you will come to understand that what you think has been your greatest **affliction**, has really been your **greatest gift**. My understanding of this "gift" called **addiction** took root at birth, and has with increasing vigor, consumed my attention for the last 40 years. My hope now is to offer you a new understanding of **how addiction operates**, **why you are walking its path**, **the purpose for it in your life**, and the comfort of knowing that you possess all the necessary components to arrive at a place where you are able to create "***a life beyond your wildest dreams"***.

Along the Path we are given the required "tools for the journey". Many of these tools have been discovered and passed down by our 12-Step predecessors, to include the need to recognize the "**Unmanageability** of our lives, our **Powerlessness** over what we cannot change, our willingness to trust that there is a **Power Greater than Ourselves**, and finally our commitment to "**Turn our lives over to the God of our Understanding"**. Whether we are in the role of addict/alcoholic or loved one, the tools are the same, and when relied upon, serve to release us from a life of physical, mental and spiritual bondage. Sometimes these "tools" will look like impossible obstacles, and other times they will provide the most profound solution at the last minute to "save us from certain destruction"..., to keep us on the Path. Ultimately they will lead us to overflowing **Gratitude**, and a new **Peace** we have never known before.

As we progress, we come to understand that:

- Our Path is always "interactive", guided by a Power Greater than Ourselves, allowing us the choices and consequences to transform our **Fear** to **Faith.**
- "**Integrity**", we learn, is as primary to our success as breath is to life, and serves as a trusty guide through the most difficult and complicated situations.
- Beyond a shadow of a doubt, we are always and forever connected to a Creator who loves us unconditionally, despite the discipline necessary for our perfect enlightenment.
- By our painstaking efforts, the Grace of our Creator, and the Path of Addiction, we experience a **purification process,** transforming our lives to **gratitude** and **joy**.

History and Meaning

The poem "*The Gift of Addiction*" was written in 2006, in response to patient, "Sean" and his reaction to a Guided Imagery exercise while in group therapy at Hemet Valley Recovery Center.

As an Adult Child of an Alcoholic father, I grew up with a general sense of mental confusion, emotional pain, and an unconscious fear that I didn't belong "here". This vague sense was accompanied by a "knowing" that if I could just "see behind the curtain", it would all make sense and I could understand where and who I was. Along the Path through my own tests and gifts, kicking and screaming, I was ultimately, and over many years, brought to the understanding that Surrender was the necessary attitude I must adopt to survive. Seemingly absurd as a viable solution, getting to Surrender, and staying there, requires conquering nearly impossible obstacles..., which the Path of Addiction graciously offers. Lessons encountered along this Path include Fear, Heartbreak, Denial, Anger, Betrayal, Shame, Remorse, Guilt, Worry, Judgment, Loss, and a myriad of other Darknesses. After having gained sufficient Self-Discipline and Faith through surviving these seemingly impossible obstacles, we ultimately come to understand the reason behind the strict AA Big Book requirement to "*Surrender to a Power Greater than Myself*", as a preventative measure for returning to the Dark. We see how addiction works..., without due diligence, it stealthily and reliably draws Addicts and Alcoholics back to relapse, and relapse to potential destruction. The Gift of Addiction is the PURIFICATION process, which in due course, magnetizes a *"life beyond our wildest dreams"*. Call it God's Grace, Karma, or Divine Providence, we ultimately find that our ability to Surrender results in the Gifts of Love, Faith, Joy, Honesty, Forgiveness, and Gratitude, in spite of the chaos and confusion present in the world. Ever returning to the familiar Darknesses of Addiction, therefore becomes much too great a price to pay. Soon these Darknesses fade into the recesses of our memory, leaving only the LIGHT. (Gift! ☺)

Addiction (as a spiritual path) requires ultimate INTEGRITY and alignment with LIGHT Energy to prevent the darkness from prevailing.

Author's Story

I was born in Jamestown, New York on February 16, 1950, to a locally prominent family of English, Scottish and Welsh descent. My grandfather, on my mother's side was a staunch businessman who owned, and with exacting authority, oversaw the development and management of numerous furniture factories throughout the northeast. As a civic minded individual, he also assumed public service roles within the municipality. My grandmother was equally visible and actively engaged in the many charitable activities of the day, her life being strictly governed by societal expectations. Two children were born of this marriage, one of them being my mother. Although my father had a tremendous influence on my life, it was my mother who gave me the greatest wisdom through her unceasing, and often failed attempts to "domesticate" her unruly daughter.

Formality took on a new definition in our family – manners, speech and presentation were emphasized above all else. How one behaved and appeared outwardly was paramount to any other unique personality characteristic that may have been stored on the inside. Our environment was an example of a perfect department store window – with all the trimmings, ALL THE TIME. Every night, dinner was a formal affair, announced and delivered with absolute perfection. Although we may not have known just what it was on our plate, we did our best to appear gracious to my mother and the cook who had, once again planned, prepped and presented a King's fare. I have memories of luscious meals, fine china and silver, and my brother trying to make me giggle. I was the one who always tried to respect the formality, and at the same time protect my brother from mother's stern gaze, and her disdain at our disruptive behavior. Thus, this was the energy that comprised the atmosphere of our home. Many years later, I was able to understand my role, as defined in addictive family systems, as the HERO, and my brother as the SCAPEGOAT. **Control** was the ultimate state of the environment - to be maintained at all costs.

As I grew older, I escaped the "mold" through an avid interest in horseback riding. This became my love and my outlet for all my growing-up years. Although somewhat reproved because I could not play the part of socialite or intellectual, I was ultimately saved because the equestrian sport held an equivalent positive rating in my parent's circles. Therefore, my life, except for my studies, was spent primarily at the stables – every day, every waking hour. Life was good. I lived in my riding clothes, no dresses; my boots full of manure - in heaven! And my parents were 100% supportive in every way. My brother was young, innocent and happy, but there was only one increasing problem – my father's drinking.

I remember becoming aware of **Fear** when I observed him with that "cocktail" in his hand. Then came the fights between my parents, when beneath my covers, I would pray to God that they would stop arguing. I remember the **Fear** – not breathing, shaking, shivering, and crying myself to sleep. Although our parents loved my brother and me dearly, the outward expression of affection primarily presented itself in my father. He was my shining star; always the one to encourage me, support me, and love me unconditionally. He was funny and smart, good-looking and a friend to all. Always social, my father could talk to anyone about anything. However, he was ruled, judged, and controlled by my mother and her parents. Enough was never enough – this I came to understand at a later age when my grandfather "removed" my father from our home. My brother and I never heard our mother say his name again. No explanations – just the understanding that our father was not to be discussed, or ever welcome in our family again ..., period. **Denial** and keeping **Secrets** took a prominent position on my stage. Thus began my nightmare and my struggle.

As any HERO will understand, I felt responsible for holding everything together in our family. If there was any outward evidence of conflict, I went directly to task to resolve and repair. Many Adult Children of Alcoholics (ACOA's) share the same experience. **Fear** was the "internal taskmaster" that drove me to feel responsible for other people's feelings, and basically everything else in my environment – and the HERO's job took on primary importance. My **"mask"** of being **capable** and in **control** was firmly established.

As I grew up, I did not have the understanding, desire or inclination to meet the expectations that my mother, and her mother, and her mother, and society had set for me. Because of this horrible flaw, I held a secret **Guilt** and feeling of **Failure**. I really never "fit in" and now the evidence was right in front of my face. My father was gone – and he was VERY sick. My horses could not heal me – nothing could heal me. I was 19 years old, lost and scared.

As values go, my birth family taught me many wonderful things, and in retrospect, I cherish those values as much today as I disliked them while growing up. Ingrained in me were three predominant ideas: **Good Manners**, **Responsibility** and **Perfection**. These, beside their cousins **Neatness**, **Cleanliness**, **Beauty**, and **Efficiency** have always run alongside my trail of many forks. An inherent quality I have always possessed is **Determination** – the "Big Sister" I have looked up to and counted on in the hardest of times – though occasionally emerging as **Self Will**, her toes stubbed and bloody.

Integrity was not something I could have defined while growing up, but **Lack of Integrity** was predominant in my early environment. I did not have any reference for understanding it, except within my father. Although unpopular with my mother and her family at times, my father always spoke the truth – he typically fractured the facade behind which "appropriateness" stanchly resided. Therefore, **Appropriateness** and **Integrity** took their places as primary characteristics within my being at a very young age.

Though **Gratitude** and **Forgiveness** were present, and always nearby, I didn't acknowledge their price or value until much later in my life. To this day, they have been the hardest won gifts. **Faith** was never something I thought much about because my family never spoke of it. However, with no attachment to any teaching or Higher Being, I inherently possessed an unshakable knowing that a Creator existed, and had only the best plans for our existence. Knowing is different than belief in this sense – it provided an unacknowledged certainty that all would turn out well.

As a necessary counterbalance of light to dark, added to these ingredients were the Black Sheep neighbors of **Fear**, **Judgment**, **Guilt** and **Shame**. Sprinkled and infused within my consciousness like a dirty ozone layer, they became permanent residents, always close by to invade and destroy. Their company was fundamental to the ultimate strategy of "God." They provided the conditions necessary to engage in the battle ahead.

So goes the tapestry whose picture only became visible in small increments over a long period of time, for which the value of **Endurance** was necessary. **Endurance** is not something I possessed or understood. My beloved father was the catalyst for the necessity of its application, and all that was to come. His alcoholism drove a wedge between us. He became isolated in **Anger**, **Isolation** and **Regret**. I became engulfed in **Fear**. Knowing nothing in those days about Alcoholics Anonymous or ALANON, we moved into separation, both trying to survive lost dreams. My path led me to exiting society altogether – his led to an alcoholic death at age 49.

I suppose I could say that if the use of drugs and/or alcohol were to be part of my path, they would have shown up at this point to temporarily assist me. However, I was never drawn to either, but was rather quite afraid of any "foreign substance". I did however, have an experience with marijuana that you might find interesting. Prior to my "exit", I was given a marijuana "joint" by my best girlfriend, who said I should "try it." Three puffs later I was choking and sputtering. Enough of that! So I threw it in the toilet and flushed it away, thinking how stupid it was because it did nothing for me! Then strangely, in the middle of the day, I lay down on the couch. Before long, my mind was engaged in the most interesting discourse on all subjects I could imagine. The only way I can describe the experience is to say that anything I thought about, I knew everything about, and the "knowing" was spontaneous – from one subject to another. I do not know how long this lasted before I fell asleep, or how long I slept. But, when I woke up and reflected on what had happened, something in me had transformed. I was unsure what it was, but I knew that who I used to be was no longer who I was. I also knew another vital point – nothing is as we think it to be. This experience was the catalyst. It provided the **Courage** to step outside the white picket fence. (However, I understood at some level, that the marijuana experience was a gift not to be abused.)

Intuition must be mentioned here. With arrows pointed in all directions, we somehow choose a path. I believe our path, although typically questioned at every step along the way, is undeniably guided and divinely fulfilled for our ultimate purpose and **Life Lessons**. Like the tapestry from underneath looking jumbled and messy, our lives take on a chaotic semblance of apparent disorganization and misdirection. Our parents and superiors have much to say about what we should and shouldn't do, but we intuitively do as we are internally guided to do – popular with others or not.

Little did I understand the impact of my father's drinking on my outlook and future, or the impact it had on my psychic equilibrium. Although I had become a successful riding instructor and trainer at the stables where I had ridden since I was 7 years old, I chose to give up my students, my horses, my friends, and my planned future, to go to Canada and "live in the woods", all the while knowing that my mother would feel that this was a highly inappropriate choice for someone with my upbringing and life standards (really meaning *her* upbringing and life standards.) Nonetheless, off I went with few possessions, internally guided to my destination of Northern British Columbia, Canada to seek out the "Doukhobors". The Doukhobor movement emerged in 18th century Russia as a Christian peasant reaction to the excessive opulence and ritualistic authority of the Orthodox Church. Doukhobors practiced a simpler form of religion, rejecting the literal Bible and the need for an intermediary priesthood, looking inward within themselves for the Voice of God. (Further information about the Doukhobors can be found at http://www.usccdoukhobors.org/about.htm#)

Factors leading up to the radical decision to leave my comfortable "American life" and "join" the Doukhobors felt definitely out of my control - so much out of my control that what I was choosing to do emerged in a sequence of experiences that I did not seek out in any way. Some of my memories of those days come to mind: Living in a log cabin in a cow pasture with access only by raft - learning how to cut wood, grow a garden, tend goats, eat out of the woods, bake bread and become resourceful with everything in nature. But most memorable to me was the **Integrity** and natural **Spirituality** of the Doukhobors. So simple they were, yet their lives so profound. I found in them a like spirituality inside myself that was completely foreign, yet comfortable and familiar at the same time. Being in their company brought new, yet old insights and dreams to my memory – some taking form, others like misty fragrances. I was changed and charged with new energy and excitement, both of which I would need an abundance of to continue along my way.

Many scary and wonderful things happened along this path. My aforementioned Black Sheep neighbors of **Fear**, **Judgment**, **Guilt** and **Shame** were challenged for the lingering predominance they intended to maintain within my consciousness. Many bloody internal battles ensued over the next 5 years, seemingly never to end. My great feelings of independence fought with my **Guilt** of irresponsibility. My new feeling of freedom fought with my **Fear** of returning to the world. My understanding of what was good and right fought with my **Judgment** of myself and others, and my wonderful feeling of liberation fought with my **Shame** for abandoning my family. Many days and nights were spent in tears of confusion, with **Fear** at the helm. My feelings of "disconnection" became very frightening - I felt no connection to anything in, or of this world, nor did I have any desire to participate in its seemingly endless dichotomies. Not really possessing any true identity, all I could ask was: Who am I? Where did I come from? Who made me? What place is this? What am I to do here? When can I come home? And where is that? Is there a God who knows me? Where are You?

While out in nature, I had the freedom to "sense" God. I typically do not mentally store facts - it is the energy from the facts that sticks with me. So, throughout my life, any facts about Jesus or God had translated into feelings only. My feelings were now somehow anticipatory – waiting for something. But rudely, my rational mind would kick in and say, "God is not going to talk to you! What are you thinking?" I spent countless hours, days, weeks, months and years pondering. How could my existence be explained? It all seemed too painful and confusing. I was too small and insignificant to ever understand.

It was winter in the year 1971 when I found myself especially vulnerable. It was no particular night, or particular experience that day that put me to bed feeling this way. I just remember thinking that nothing was more important than God. I never understood any of the Christian scriptures, and had no real connection to Jesus Christ, but somehow I knew that he was very close to God. These were the thoughts that followed me to bed that night in the log cabin. I remember climbing into my sleeping bag in the loft and drifting off to sleep. The next thing I remember is so difficult to describe...

I sat straight up in my sleeping bag and "knew" that God was in the room. As simple and crazy as that!! I think I sat there stunned and somewhat scared – but I knew it was God. I said nothing and He said nothing - everything was communicated intuitively. It could have been a minute or an hour. There was no time. At some point my head found the pillow again, and it was not until I opened my eyes in the morning that I remembered what happened the night before.

In the stark daylight it seemed the experience must certainly have been a dream – not something that actually happened. The review and analysis became my total focus. What I can say for sure, is that God let me know of His presence and filled me with a kind of new energy – like dancing bubbles on water. What I cannot tell you is anything that was said. Spiritual experiences are said to be like that – nonsensical when they are expressed. But this was mine, and why it happened on that night, and in that way I do not know. I just know that I have never ever forgotten it – like it happened yesterday, 40 years ago.

What was I to do now? Once again I had that anticipatory feeling, but it was like holding onto a cloud. However, there was a new "**Knowing**" that I was not alone, and that Someone knew my heart and my struggles. Someone "bigger than life" was going out in front of me - who I was to follow. This feeling sustained me day and night. I found such joy in just thinking about it. The "bubbles" would return at the thought of Him- like the feeling in High School when I had a new date.

Years passed. Long days were spent in the garden, chopping wood for winter, and watching the goats perilously jump from one rock to another in the wild, raging river. Occasionally I had to stock up on staple supplies by going into town. This was a major undertaking that only happened 3-4 times a year. The little money I had provided for adequate amounts of rice, soy beans, split peas, lentils, rolled oats, raisins, almonds, flour, yeast, sugar, molasses, olive oil, kerosene and soap. With the addition of fresh vegetables in the summer and root vegetables in the winter, physical needs were nicely met.

On one such trip to the Whole Foods store in town, I happened upon a dusty old bookstore next door. Once inside, I found many rooms of endless shelves and tables piled high and packed tightly with new and used books of every kind. One could get lost forever in all the pages, I thought. Glancing at a large round table, piled high with books of every size, I noticed that the blue book on top was about to fall off, which could ultimately cause a serious avalanche. Reaching over to rebalance the mountain of books, I glanced at the title of the blue book, *"Autobiography of a Yogi"*, and thought, "What is a Yogi?" Somehow I couldn't put the book down. I looked for the price and found it inside the front cover - $3.65. Well…, I certainly didn't have that kind of money, so the Yogi understanding would have to wait. Moving through the rest of the bookstore with my mind still on the blue book, I finally exited, got in my truck, started the engine, stopped the engine, got out, went back into the store, bought the book – then, headed home. My life was never the same from that day on. The Yogi mentioned in the title is Paramahansa Yogananda. He has now been my spiritual teacher for 43 years.

Fast forward…, with my new spiritual companionship, I was unintentionally yet systematically returned to my hometown, Jamestown, NY to "face the music", which I knew would not be melodious if I didn't drop my **Opinions** and **Judgments.** My **Attitude** HAD to change if I were to rejoin my family. Many discussions ensued at my return, most of which were frustrating because it seemed impossible to explain to the "rationally minded", WHY I had chosen to live in Canada as a primitive barbarian! It was easier for them to **Deny** it had all happened rather than **Accept** what they couldn't understand. Soon I realized that there were no logical answers that would suffice to provide them with an objective understanding, so I decided that my new life would begin with a list of **Action** items, which would temporarily defer any further discussions and potential, fatal misunderstandings regarding how I had "lost my mind" and hoped to find it again. These items included where I would live and what I would do. Somehow, as if out of the blue, I said to my mother, "I know what I am going to do! I am going to go to Nursing School!" This was said as if I had planned it for years. (Never before had I even thought about attending Nursing School, or for that matter, becoming a Nurse) Within the week, I was enrolled in a Registered Nursing program to begin in September, and moved into the upstairs flat of a building owned by my new stepfather. How could this happen so easily? Why weren't the multitudes condemning me for my deplorable absence? Why was my mother and new step-family so kind and helpful? (Gifts! ☺)

In 1977 I graduated with honors as a Registered Nurse, and married a man I had known since we were in Junior High School. Soon after that I accepted my first nursing job at the local hospital – on the Psychiatric Unit! I was in seventh heaven because I could TALK to the patients. Perfect!! Perfect until I was informed that there was a "Chemical Dependency Program" on the unit as well - Chemical Dependency? You mean drugs and ALCOHOL? Oh never! I can't possibly work on this floor. Please let me OUT! Well, once again, God had other plans.

I was to begin my career treating alcoholics and addicts and on that day; facing my GREATEST **Fear** – the deadly disease that killed my father. **Trust** and **Faith** became my only lifeline – I was terrified of alcoholism. I was not only terrified of it, but felt an overwhelming personal **Guilt** and **Shame** associated with it. (Not sure why?) How could I ever be therapeutic with the patients? No other nursing jobs were available within the hospital. So, I took the job – on the night shift! With the support, patience and encouragement of the many healthcare professionals I have had the honor to work with, I have now been working with addicts and alcoholics since that early beginning in 1977. Throughout the years, I have learned all I know about addiction from our patients, God, and my Spiritual Teacher. Having had the opportunity to work on the front lines of psychiatric and chemical dependency treatment with both adults and adolescents, my roles included many years as a Staff Nurse, then the opportunity to manage a Multiple Personality Disorder Unit, and then to assume numerous Senior Management roles.

Throughout, I was searching for an understanding, an identity, a “knowing” that all human conditions were assigned for our greatest good. To gain this understanding, many difficult tests, obstacles, and challenges presented themselves, including how to maintain **Integrity** in a healthcare system that had become a business. Business and Service are not always compatible – so therefore, God used that discrepancy as a backdrop for the ongoing battle of **Fear** and **Faith** to continue with gusto in my life. Without the security of a **Spiritual Path,** I would not have had the courage to challenge some members of Hospital Leadership who placed “bottom line” priority over patient care. Being extremely uncomfortable in addressing my peers and superiors with issues of their own **Integrity**, and fearful of what such conflict could cause within the organization, I would typically try to **Deny** the obvious – until in doing so, MY own **Integrity** became shaky. This was unacceptable! So, as God would have it, I HAD to turn to Him, in other words, **Surrender** my will to a **Power Greater than Myself**. Hours were spent in **Meditation** imploring God to please “fix” the situation, and guide me to the best thing I should do. Do I stay and fight? Or, do I leave on principal? These challenges were my bane, and kept me awake many nights, until one particular night. The message I intuitively received was, *“All things are necessary, the good and the bad, the fear and the faith, the joy and the sorrow, the old and the new, the young and the old, the light and the dark. All that is needed is your* ***Acceptance****, and then your* ***Agreement with your decision*** *to take a certain course. Your* ***Ambivalence*** *has been the source of your own conflict.”* WOW!!

As this fundamental understanding took form in my mind, my career challenges became easier, although not absent for sure! I am still confronted with subtle (or not so subtle) situations that require "**doing the right thing for the right reason**" unpopular, painful or not! This philosophy, being the "rock" upon which I stand as a nurse, clinician, and hospital leader, affords me, the patients, and the staff the "recovery" we all require every day as addicts, alcoholics, co-dependents, and practitioners of the "12 Steps of AA".

I continue to implore God for the clarity to see through the baffling, cunning and powerful manifestations of the Dark side of Duality, while always reminding myself that this earthly environment and our experience of it is perfectly choreographed and orchestrated by our "Divine Producer and Director", and all is eternally well.

GIFTS

In retrospect I can see how the events of our lives have followed an intelligent and purposeful sequence. Our intelligent God does not put us into situations for which we have no aptitude, or the tools necessary to survive them. Sometimes however, I have questioned the many complexities of my career experience, and wondered if I would ever truly feel accomplished or comfortable as a Nurse Leader in a health care system that frequently seems so impersonal and detached from the hearts of humanity. Throughout the years, I have found that the only answer to the dilemma of my frustration is to **Surrender** to the current moment. To do this successfully requires **Effort**, **Self-Discipline**, and commitment to a **Spiritual Practice**. To my Spiritual Practice I have added one **Prayer**, a prayer that always keeps me out of trouble, and on the right path.

My prayer is:

"No Questions,

No Complaints,

At Your Service."

In addition to this prayer, the daily practice of Meditation has been essential as a reminder of our greater spiritual reality, my identity as a soul, and the life purpose for which I am here. Through God given instruction and meditation techniques, I have received the Gift of a solid spiritual foundation upon which to depend - which is also magically in harmony with the 12 Step philosophy. (Gift! ☺)

Through the American Holistic Nurse's Association, I received Board Certification in 2001 as a Holistic Nurse. This certification has provided the professional credibility to incorporate into our treatment of chemically dependent patients the practice of yoga, meditation, energy healing, chakra therapy, acupuncture, and other holistic modalities. (Gift! ☺)

"The Gift of Addiction" took form as we fast forward to the year 2006. Utilizing the following Guided Imagery script (author unknown), Sean, a male patient in the group, had a profound experience from the exercise.

Who You Really Are..........

Take a deep breath
Quiet your body
Quiet your thoughts
Quiet your breath
Let it all go...

Now, as you rest in this peaceful place...

- Sense who you are without this room
- Sense who you are without your current circumstances
- Sense who you are without your parents
- Sense who you are without your friends
- Sense who you are without your career
- Sense who you are without judgments about others
- Sense who you are without judgments about yourself
- Sense who you are without judgments about the world
- Sense who you are without your eyesight
- Sense who you are without your hearing
- Sense who you are without your ability to touch, taste or smell
- Sense who you are without your ability to speak
- Sense who you are without your ability to think
- Sense who you are without your body
- Sense who you are without your breath
- Sense who you are without your pain
- Sense who you are apart from all these things

Allow this sense to come to you as it will,
without pushing or resisting.

Now, holding your paper and pen, sit comfortably with your eyes closed. Take three deep breaths through your nose, exhaling through your mouth. Let the muscles of your neck and back relax with each exhale, feeling your shoulders drop and your weight settle in the bottom of your body. Continue to follow the inhale and exhale of your breath; the rising and falling of your body. If thoughts come, simply acknowledge them and let them go, bringing your attention back to your breath. Now, ask yourself. "Who am I?" "What is the truest statement I can say about myself?"

When you are ready, and without judgment, pick up your paper and pen and write the statement that comes. Then close your eyes and gently sit with it.

What feelings does this statement elicit? What thoughts? Be with any thoughts or feelings that come without being caught in them – just being the observer.

Now ask yourself if there is a statement you could write that would be truer than the one you have written, if so, what is it? Write it. If not, simply stay with the statement you have written. Repeat this process with any new statements that come, simply sitting with the truth you know about yourself, without judgment.

After you have completed this process, take another breath, and reaching into the deepest part of your soul ask again, "Who am I?" "What is the truest statement I can write about myself?" Write it.

Sean

Sean, a 31 year old male patient was admitted for medical detoxification from Alcohol, Methamphetamines and Marijuana. His detoxification process was proceeding successfully by day 3, with no complicating medical or psychiatric problems however, he presented in group as very guarded, and resistive. His dress and appearance was that of a "biker", and included many tattoos, leather outerwear, body piercings, etc. His eye contact was minimal, and his body language screamed, "Don't get near me!" As is my general practice at the beginning of each group, I go from patient to patient, taking their hands in acknowledgement, and individually greet them. When I came to Sean, he physically recoiled, and blurted out, "Don't touch me!!" I accepted his request and stepped back. Over the next few days, he remained hostile, reclusive and non-interactive with staff and his peers. It was on a Wednesday that I introduced the above Guided Imagery into the group process – he was sitting in the back right corner of the room throughout the exercise. I handed each patient 3 blank paper cards to write on for the exercise, and I was shocked that he was actually writing.

After about 5 minutes, I asked if any of the patients wanted to share what they had written on their cards. In scanning the room, I looked over at Sean and observed that he was crying. Not being unusual for this type of emotional release to be exhibited during the group process, I was nonetheless shocked to see that it was he who was crying. Somehow, I intuitively felt safe in approaching him, and as I did he reached out and began hugging me like a child. He wept and wept until another patient offered him a tissue, at which point he wiped his eyes, blew his nose and sat back in his chair.

I asked him, "Sean, would you like to share your experience with the group?" to which he reluctantly replied, "The truest statement I can say about myself is that **"I am a child of God."** The room was silent but electrified by his offering - all patients were visibly touched, as was I.

The exercise took him temporarily out of his Pain enough to remember who he really was. This and many other modalities like it are incorporated into the healing of the addict. As I drove home that night, I couldn't get Sean out of my mind. Having practiced in this field for many years, I have learned to set healthy personal and work boundaries, and typically do not "ruminate" about patients once I leave the hospital. By the time I got home (1-1/2 hour commute) I still couldn't get him out of my mind. Somehow I found myself at my computer writing furiously, without stopping to even see what I was writing. The following is the result of that effort; an effort that was not my own and did not come from me. It came from a part inside of me that connected with a divine intelligence - as a channel.

The Gift of Addiction

ADDICTION SAYS:

I will make you lie, cheat and steal
I will take your self-respect
I will take your confidence
I will take your family
I will take your children
I will take your livelihood
I will ruin your body
I will take your sleep
I will derange your mind
I will take your memory
I will take your joy
I will take your courage
I will take your creativity
I will take your heart
I will take your love
I will take your energy
I will take your power
I will take your intelligence
I will take your enthusiasm
I will take your humor
I will take your intuition
I will take your compassion
I will take your integrity
I will take your gratitude
I will take your faith
I will take your trust
I will take your dreams
I will take your hope
I will take your wisdom

I AM A GIFT LIKE NO OTHER, AND IF YOU DON'T STOP ME …
I will take your life.

BUT, IN THE PROCESS OF MY DESTRUCTION OF YOU …

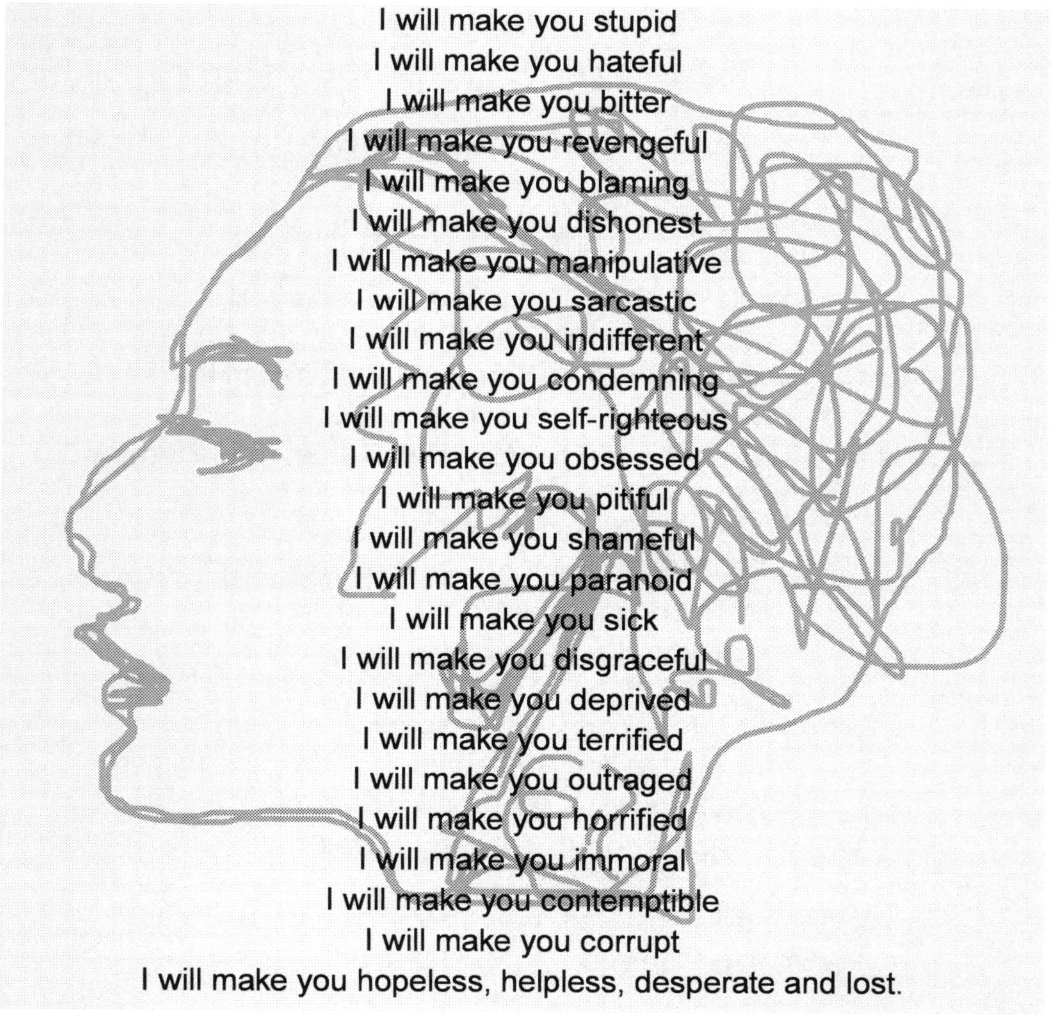

I will make you stupid
I will make you hateful
I will make you bitter
I will make you revengeful
I will make you blaming
I will make you dishonest
I will make you manipulative
I will make you sarcastic
I will make you indifferent
I will make you condemning
I will make you self-righteous
I will make you obsessed
I will make you pitiful
I will make you shameful
I will make you paranoid
I will make you sick
I will make you disgraceful
I will make you deprived
I will make you terrified
I will make you outraged
I will make you horrified
I will make you immoral
I will make you contemptible
I will make you corrupt
I will make you hopeless, helpless, desperate and lost.

WHAT YOU DON'T KNOW ABOUT ME IS THAT I AM YOUR GREATEST GIFT, SENT TO YOU FROM GOD.

GOD SAYS:

<u>I Am Unrelenting</u>

You See, My Dear, Dear Child, I Love You.
How Else Can I Guarantee To You That You Will Know
Who You Really Are?
<u>Addiction Is The Guarantee</u>

You Must See Who You Are Not
To Understand Who You Are
<u>Addiction Is The Guarantee</u>

There Is No Other Way Out Of Addiction
I Am the Only Door
To Go Through the Door You Must Find Your Heart
Love and Only Love Is the Key
There Is Much About Love That You Will Come To Understand

There Is No Other Way Out
You Will Remember Who You Are
By Experiencing Who You Are Not
<u>Addiction Is The Guarantee</u>

This Was Our Agreement
Do You Remember?
Addiction Was My Promise to You
<u>Addiction Is The Guarantee</u>

We Agreed To This Path Way Before You Were Born
With Much Planning, Organizing and Excitement

YOUR SOUL HAS ALWAYS KNOWN THIS, ONLY YOUR MIND HAS FORGOTTEN…. AS WAS THE PLAN

You Must Remember Only A Few Vital Things:

I Love You
Talk To Me
Listen To Me in the Silence
Everything Is Perfect, Just As We Planned It to Be
See My Face In All Faces… Faces Who Know, Faces Who Don't
You Cannot Make a Mistake
Service to the Enlightenment of Others
Will Hasten Your Enlightenment
You Are Always Loved, Guided and Protected
You Are Eternal, You Cannot Die

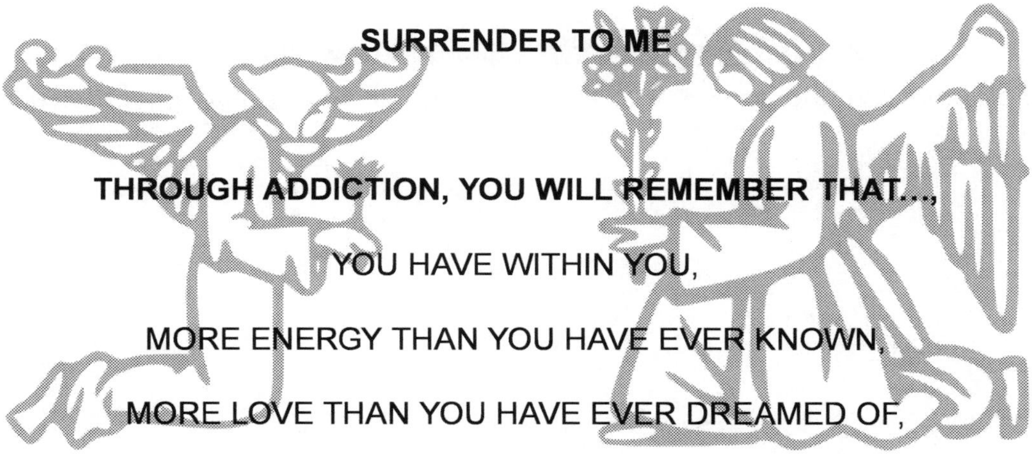

SURRENDER TO ME

THROUGH ADDICTION, YOU WILL REMEMBER THAT…,

YOU HAVE WITHIN YOU,

MORE ENERGY THAN YOU HAVE EVER KNOWN,

MORE LOVE THAN YOU HAVE EVER DREAMED OF,

MORE TALENT THAN YOU HAVE EVER IMAGINED,

MORE STRENGTH THAN YOU HAVE EVER HOPED FOR,

MORE JOY THAN YOU HAVE EVER FANCIED,

AND MORE TO GIVE THAN YOU HAVE EVER GIVEN.

THIS IS MY PROMISE TO YOU,

SURRENDER TO ME.

After completing those last three words, no further material was funneled into my mind – all was peaceful, still, and calm. Apparently…., the "work" was complete. Not actually remembering what had been written, I took the time to read the entire piece, reflecting on each word thinking, this is very powerful, where did this information come from? Why did it come to me…in this way, tonight? Exhausted, and not having the energy to ponder further, I went upstairs to bed…, my bed, familiar and predictable, to close my eyes and empty my head. But one word stuck tight to my whole being as I fell asleep - that word was **SURRENDER**. It has since taken up permanent residence with ever increasing authority, as the chief manager, supervisor and organizer of my life. And if I EVER assume to proceed independently, I am reminded, sooner or later, that God is the doer, not me!!

Since its origin, *The Gift of Addiction*, has been introduced to hundreds of patients with the same response - Awe, Relief, and Gratitude. (Gift! ☺)

The following is in response to the
Cautionary Warnings and **Threats of Loss**
identified in "**The Gift of Addiction**"
by **Personal Accounts** from
Addicts and **Alcoholics** who are now
striving for a "**Life of Recovery**" ☺

ADDICTION SAYS…

I will take your Courage - "I could not stand up for what I thought was right. I tried to put the pieces of my life together but I could never complete the puzzle. I tried to "step up" for who I am but always stumbled, so I had to use alcohol."

I will take your Faith - "My Faith and God are very important to me – it is a huge part of who I am. Losing that, and feeling the Spirit slowly leaving my body made me feel so Dark and Alone."

I will take your Intelligence - "The mental capacity that I had left me with emptiness, and "dumbed me down" to the point of becoming a part of the ground. Addiction numbed my mind and my heart – it was running me farther away - I was scared and afraid."

I will take your Compassion - "My compassion was taken by Heroin addiction, and by my actions because I cared about nothing but putting a needle in my arm. I didn't care about who I hurt, who I crossed, or who I killed. Especially, I had no compassion when it came to slowly killing myself."

I will take your Trust - "Addiction took my trust in God, family, myself, and life itself. Addiction took me to the Dark Ruins of heroin addiction. I call it the "Black Plague".

I will take your Wisdom - "When I was younger, people often commented that I was mature, intelligent and wise for my age. I have always held positions requiring a B.A. or Master's Degree, without ever having any college degree at all. And yet, after 8 years of sobriety I relapsed. Then after a terrible detox and a 30-day program, I decided that I could manage 1 glass of wine. Fast forward 1 year later, I am drinking a fifth of vodka daily." I am now 51, with a broken shoulder in 3 places…, so once again I decide to get help. On my way to rehab, I decide to drink the "last pint I will ever have". I wake up in jail with no memory of how I got there. How "Wise" is it to argue with the police when you're intoxicated?"

I will take your Sleep - "So many nights I couldn't stop thinking – worried about things I had no control over - always worried about running out of pills, and possibly getting sick at work. Worried about my husband finding out I was taking opiates again – he threatened divorce the last time I relapsed. Going to my underwear drawer, I took out a hidden bottle of vodka and snuck into the bathroom - I have to work tomorrow."

I will take your Children - "I am Addiction, I took your children. I left a deep, dark hole inside of you. A twisted, agonizing pain in the pit of your stomach that is relentless. You won't stop crying. Your heart will break from missing them. I WILL NEVER STOP! Only your God can save you now!"

I will take your Joy - "With "using", Joy begins to slip away. Should I want relief? I must pay for it with pieces of my happiness and sobriety. It leaves me with no sunny days, no smiling faces, no sound of laughter. It allows only poison and darkness to seep in every crack of my fragile shell."

I will make you Horrified -"Alcohol caused me to believe I was a good person. I almost killed a friend and myself."

I will take your Enthusiasm - "Addiction takes my Enthusiasm for life away day after day. I have anxiety as soon as I open my eyes, until I fall asleep at night. Anxiety has control of every thought in my head, so that I don't have time to dream of a better life.

I will take your Integrity - "I always thought I held myself to a high standard. The drinking led me to take a bottle of wine that wasn't charged to me. I also went to the liquor store with my pajamas on."

I will take your Confidence - "Now that I have been drinking again for 5 years, each year alcohol took more and more of my Confidence. Now I don't want to talk or meet anyone. They used to call me "Miss Sunshine."

I will derange your mind - "When I first came to A.A. I didn't think I needed to be restored to sanity, but in fact, I had been doing the same thing over and over again, but expecting different results. I couldn't see my Deranged Mind for the addiction."

I will take your Self Respect - "Losing my self-respect and respect of others sent me into a deep black hole. The hate for myself and lack of self-respect made me ugly."

I will ruin your Body - "I look down, see the blood, see the knife, the cut, the deep red flood. I say good-bye, can't bear to stay, for with my life I am willing to pay. I don't know how it got this bad…, I just don't know. Fast asleep I'd like to nod, and wake up no more till you are gone. My scars are deep and they are many. My body is tired, the damage is plenty. You've done your job, you got your way, but with you "friend", I cannot stay."

I will take your Memory - "Alcohol has taken many things from me, but the scariest is my memory. I can remember things from ages 2 or 3, but I can't recall what I said or did this week. I find that now I have trouble spelling simple words – even after 30 years in high level management. I had my first black-out in 2016 – people had to tell me how I ended up in County Jail. Please God, give me the strength to deal with the demons who hide at the bottom of the bottle."

I will take your Humor - "The trauma throughout my life has been pushed down – inward. I believed focusing on positive things and professional success would be enough. Once funny and positive, through my addiction, I became depressed, anxious, sad, and even mean at times to the people I love the most. Now it's hard to laugh and make others laugh when you feel negative, tired, helpless and hopeless. Alcohol stole my joy and my ability to see beauty in the world, and people."

I will take your Livelihood - "You flirted with me for years, until I couldn't resist. We had a full-blown romance for a few years, and I loved you more than anything. You veiled my perception, left me angry, confused and hopeless. You bullied me into a false sense of security, allowing me to believe I could manage a few drinks. I lost clarity at work and in my personal life. Once you had me securely in your grasp, you began to betray me. Shaking and feeling sick daily, I didn't have a choice anymore.

I chose you over work. You took my dream-job away. You took my self-respect and integrity. You left me broken."

I will take your Power - "Lost in circles of insanity, broken down and completely weak, drained of all my strength, my faith caved in, leaving no trace of me."

I will make you Contemptible - "I always made excuses for my addiction – it ran in my family so it wasn't my fault. But deep down inside of me was a terrible guilt that never left me alone. I had to make myself feel better by thinking and saying mean things about other people. It got so bad that I just hated everybody, but secretly mostly myself. My constant dark moods cost me two marriages, and still I couldn't see it was the addiction that was making me so miserable."

I will make you Obsessed - "This anxiety has me obsessed over trying to fake being happy and normal."

I will make you Outraged - "Because of my drug use, if nothing goes my way - OUTRAGE!! I always want it "my way or the highway!"

I will make you Sick - "This disease breaks your mind, body, and soul until you feel helpless and hopeless. Drinking not to get sick, but it's the drink that made you sick. Crazy? Drinking not to shake, but it's the drink that made you shaky. Crazy? You want to stop but your body has betrayed you too. If I stop now, I might have a seizure and die. I am so desperate, I cry out to God… PLEASE HELP ME LORD, I can't do it without you!"

I will make you Sarcastic - "I make you Unapproachable and Dramatic. I make you Hateful and Sarcastic. I make you Snippy, Rude and Mean. I make you Cocky, Loud, and Obscene. They all just want to stay away. They avoid your presence throughout the day - you and I, just how it should be. I will take you for mine, just wait and see."

I will make you Corrupt - "Taking money from the church, I felt paranoid all the time. I pictured God with tears in His eyes – feeling like I'm really going to Hell now! Selling my Norcos made me feel paranoid and made me feel like a drug dealer."

I will make you Bitter - "Each time drugs took something from me, I would be resentful. Now that I have nothing to lose it has made me bitter because I allowed drugs to do this to me. My addiction to drugs took people, places and things and left me empty. In sobriety I had a good job, respect from my peers, owned my own home, my car was paid for, and I had a loving relationship. After using for 5 years, I have NONE of these things – just guilt and regret.

I will make you Self-Righteous - "In addiction it is imperative that I have my own way. Everything must be in place so I can drink without distraction or interruption. To make this happen I will argue, debate, dispute, condescend, patronize, and be superior just to convince you that I am right. I am always right, and you were absurd to even question me!"

I will make you Lie, Cheat and Steal - "This addiction got me to the point of sitting in an alley, dirty, disgusting, homeless, hungry, heart broken, scarred from war, putting a needle in my arm, lying to myself.

I will make you Lost - "LOST on the lonely Island of Addiction. My plane crashed which started my addiction to prescription medications. Addiction is a Grim Reaper with a Smile, and the skill of a Butcher. He carved into my heart with no thought of nurture. I will eventually die here. God, please come into my heart and restore my soul, and make me a survivor….Please God, Help me!

I will make you Revengeful - "Alcohol caused me to be drunk at work –made me act in revengeful ways to hurt my boss and co-workers because I was ALWAYS RIGHT! "Not!!"

Chapter 2

Spiritual Path

From the day we are born to the day we die, each one of us is walking a Spiritual Path. Why? Because we are Spiritual Beings with no other choice while we are here. We are initially unaware that there is any Path at all… we just function by our instincts or intuition, guided by our parents, friends, teachers, the rules of society…, and our **Karma**.

Some of us are gifted with an "inner knowing" of who we are, and what we are to do here – however, most of us are not. Taking the opportunity to further explore the idea of ongoing existence after death, we will assume that the concept of reincarnation is an accurate interpretation of the cosmic strategy to provide enough time and experience for each soul to reach maturity – or enlightenment. Many believe that it does not seem plausible that we would experience so many unresolved issues before the show would stop, the curtain would lower, and we would forget it all - never to return for the finale.

As understood by many spiritual disciplines, the concept of **Karma**, (a term for past actions and consequences, or the law of cause and effect), may provide the explanation for some of the inherent tendencies in an individual, and the unique challenges each soul faces. Strengths and weaknesses developed from past lives are identified for *experiential opportunities* in the present life, the outcome of which creates more Karma (good and bad), and so on. **Duality** (light and dark, good and bad, rich and poor, love and hate, etc.) provides the *choices* each soul is offered to live out his roles – some given, and some chosen.

A frequent question in the hearts and minds of humanity has always been why certain souls experience health and wealth, but end their lives in a tragic death, while others are very poor, but tremendously strong and healthy, and live to a ripe old age – or any other unexplainable combinations of characteristics and circumstances that create the life environment for each soul. Does this mean that the Creator favors one over another? Or is the cosmic production based only on random selection?

No reasonable answer has ever sufficed to quiet the bereaved heart of a mother who has lost her child. Was the child defective in some way? Incarnation from a spiritual state into a physical body, onto a physical plane *should* provide us with some concept of who we are, where we came from, what we are to do here, when we are going "home", and where "home" is. Unfortunately, that seems not to be the plan of our Creator – instead it is as if we got a grand dose of "amnesia", so that we could, with our inherent and well won characteristics, go forth blindly through this "**purification process**" with intuition as our only guide.

Reincarnation is one explanation for the repeated tendencies a person has, which he could not have developed in just one lifetime. For example, one individual smokes a few times and gives up cigarettes completely. Another smokes only occasionally his whole life. And another smoker progresses immediately to excessive use and dies of lung cancer. Would these habits come from just one lifetime? The idea that we have lived before, strengthening and developing positive and negative traits in ourselves, gives us hope for the continuation of our spiritual journey. That those tendencies we have (un)knowingly created by our will, or habits in the past, we can undo by healthier actions in the present, and **Surrender** to the God of Our Understanding.

We didn't get the Memo.....

Who am I?
How did I get here?
What is this place?
What am I to do here?
Where did I come from?
When am I going back?
Who are YOU?

Generally these questions don't arise in life until we have experienced enough **Stress, Loss** and **Disappointment** to cause us to look **Inward** (to the soul), instead of **Outward** (to the material world).

Addiction offers us that **OPPORTUNITY**. (Gift! ☺)

STRESS comes in many different **packages** – in many different **strengths** and **flavors.**

Stress is always the result of Fear

Minor Stress – *"I am having a "bad hair day"* (Oh! I feel vulnerable! What will others think??) or, *I am running late for my son's baseball game*" (Oh I feel awful if he is pitching and I am not there when he looks for me in the bleachers!)

Major Stress – *"CPS has just taken my children", My husband is having an affair", I stole money from my sister's account for drugs, I have been served an eviction notice, My children won't let me see my grandchildren because of my drinking, I don't remember where I was last night* (How could I have done this again?? I need my drugs/alcohol to cope right now!!)

As part of the **ADDICTIVE CYCLE**, the consequences of **Stress and Fear** will ultimately lead me to reach for **HELP!!!**

But my **DENIAL**
may be stronger than my **willingness to change**.
Therefore, I may continue drinking/using
and suffer **many more consequences**.

Stealthy, **Sneaky** and **Sly**, my addiction
Cautiously, **Covertly** and **Secretly**
progresses through my body, mind and spirit
to an **Acute, Debilitating, Fatal** condition.

THIS IS MY **Spiritual Path**
It is called "**ADDICTION"**
(I agreed to this Path way before I was born)

My **Addictive Process** has lead me to the first

"Tools on the Path"

How could substances like Alcohol, Cocaine, Meth, Heroin, Oxycontin, or Ativan - or all their family members - Percocet, Norco, Vicodin, THC, Dilaudid, Xanax, Klopopin, Fentanyl, or Valium be **"Tools on the Path"**, or EVER cause me to become their slave?

HOW?

After seeing people I know **die** of alcoholism,
or end up **prison**, or **overdose** on pills ?

A Spiritual Path must be compelling.
Addiction is compelling, and we agreed to it.

WHY?

Because, in this lifetime, we were ready to look outside
the physical box of **disappointing materiality.**

WHY?

Because somewhere deep inside of us, we knew
there was much more to the picture

BUT,

How could a substance like Alcohol, Cocaine, Meth, Heroin, Oxycontin, or Ativan - or their family members - Percocet, Norco, Vicodin, THC, Dilaudid, Xanax, Klopopin, Fentanyl, or Valium be considered

"Tools on the Path" Really?

Because they allow me to Understand Who I Am
by experiencing Who I Am Not *(Gift! ☺)*

In order for me to use them I will have to learn to
Lie, Cheat, and **Steal,** and somehow
feel that it is OK to do so.

Therein lies my dilemma…, by doing so,
I am denying **the truth of my soul**, and **my soul knows it**.
(Even though I have convinced my mind otherwise)

DENIAL… ☹

There are many other ***Spiritual Paths***
that souls agree to, not just ***ADDICTION.***

If the purpose of the "Path" is to answer these same questions:

Who am I?
How did I get here?
What is this place?
What am I to do here?
Where did I come from?
When am I going back?
Who are YOU?

Then**,** the Path has to have the same components of
Stress and **Fear** to compel us to **look within** for the answers.

Examples of other "Involuntary Spiritual Paths"
might look like:

Physical Disease
Mental Disease
Poverty
Life-changing catastrophe
Severe Physical Trauma
Death/Loss
Confinement/ Separation
Failure

Each Path however, is a **"Journey to Enlightenment"...,** because each one ultimately causes us to "<u>look within</u>", because sooner or later we understand that "<u>looking without</u>" cannot heal us.

Some Paths are more challenging than others -
ADDICTION may be the most difficult path because
"**Falling off** and **Staying off**"
can, and ultimately will
lead to **DEATH** - swift or prolonged.

Through the process of Addiction, God says,
"I WILL FORCE YOU TO FIND ME, and in finding Me, you will find Yourself." *(Gift! ☺)*

(but, the Path is Treacherous...)

Though many other **Spiritual Paths** (i.e., Severe Physical Trauma, Poverty/ Loss, Confinement/ Separation, and Failures) are "**Temporary**", and one can **"Recover"** and not return to them, the path of ADDICTION is a **Permanent "Recovering" Condition**.

Many **Lessons** along the Path deal with our **DENIAL** of this **"Permanent Condition"**, and **DENIAL** will ultimately lead to **RELAPSE.**

Many Lessons are learned through **RELAPSE.** So..., relapse must also be a **Tool on the Path!!** **AMAZING!!** (Gift! ☺)

QUESTIONS FOR PONDERING

- ♥ When did I first feel "different" from other people?
- ♥ What characteristics would I identify as "different?"
- ♥ When did I realize that I was drinking / using for other than social reasons?
- ♥ How many times have I chosen to drink/use responsibly?
- ♥ How many times have I failed?
- ♥ How many people in my "Family of Origin" would I consider alcoholics or addicts?
- ♥ How many times have I denied that I am an alcoholic/addict and been told otherwise by my closest friends or family?

- ♥ How many times have I "decided" that I am NOT an alcoholic or addict?
- ♥ Despite consequences (present or future) have I decided to drink/use?
- ♥ When did I first start to "stuff" my feelings?
- ♥ What is the weight of my Baggage? My Denial?
- ♥ Can I identify my Denial? Am I Courageous enough to do so?
- ♥ What is my Stress (Fear) Level?
- ♥ When does my Stress Level lead to Relapse?

Everyone has a Spiritual Path – Relaxed, Challenged, Rigorous, or Severe

Addiction is a **SEVERE PATH,** in other words, a matter of
Life and Death (acute or prolonged)

When walked with **Faith** and **Courage**,
it will lead to **Wisdom, Love, Joy, and Peace**,
and, ultimately to **Integrity** in this lifetime.

To arrive at **Integrity**,
(doing the right thing, at the right time, for the right reason)
one must walk through the shadows of **Suffering**,
but may not realize that **Suffering**
is a primary **TOOL** on the path.

The **Key Word** is **INTEGRITY**
(Addiction is the opposite of Integrity)

How do I get there?
More to come!! ☺

Now, let's discuss

ENERGY !

Chapter 3

Energy

Alcoholics and Addicts have a special aptitude for reading other people's **ENERGY,** or the energy in the environment, or the energy in their house, even as they drive up the driveway, before they even open the front door. (Gift! ☺)

ENERGY is the **Vibratory Quality of Duality**, meaning all the energetic qualities ranging from **Fear** to **Love** within the person, or the environment.

DUALITY refers to Opposite, or Opposing energies (Light/Dark, Good/Bad, Yes/No, etc.)

EXAMPLE: If you walk into a classroom, offering the other students no eye contact or acknowledgment, then proceed to abruptly sit down, while slamming your notebook on the table, others would easily and quickly come to the conclusion that you were **ANGRY** about something!!

That **ANGER** is powerful, contagious **ENERGY,** felt by everyone in the room, **Individually** and **Mutually** – immediately changing the **Vibratory Quality** of the environment.

ENERGY FIELDS, are both **Individual** and **Mutual,** and create the overall feeling (**vibration**) of the environment.

It is our **Thoughts** that determine our **Emotional** and **Mental** states, and also **Magnetize** similar people, experiences, and situations that correspond to our own **Energetic Nature.**

*Every **FEELING** has its own **ENERGY/ VIBRATION***

What we **think**, **say**, **intend,** and **expect** results in how we **feel.**

How we **feel** results in what we **create.**

Therefore, we **attract** by the way we **feel**.

What we **create** ultimately occurs by this **"LAW OF ATTRACTION".**

Think about someone you **LOVE** to be around.
What are the characteristics (**Energy/ Vibration**) of this person?
I bet I can guess some of them!!

LIGHT QUALITIES

Loving
Respectful
Honest
Confident
Powerful
Empathetic
Energetic
Enthusiastic
Humorous
Gentle
Caring
Grateful
Forgiving
Trustworthy
Reliable
Faithful
Flexible
Creative
Courageous
Generous
Honest
Spiritual
Humble
Authentic
Affectionate
Understanding
Insightful
Responsible
Strong

QUESTIONS:

How do you **feel** in their presence?
Who are **you,** and how do you **behave** in their presence?
Are there similarities?

Think about someone you **DO NOT LIKE** to be around.
What are the characteristics (**Energy/ Vibration**) of this person?
I bet I can guess some of them!!

DARK QUALITIES

Fearful
Angry
Self-Centered
Disrespectful
Dishonest
Lazy
Uncaring
Rude
Negative
Hateful
Entitled
Ungrateful
Unforgiving
Untrustworthy
Unreliable
Unfaithful
Rigid
Superficial
Jealous
Sarcastic
Controlling
Blaming
Unfeeling
Irresponsible
Manipulative
Bitter
Resentful
Careless
Hurtful
Pessimistic

QUESTIONS:

How do you **feel** in their presence?
Who are **you,** and how do you **behave** in their presence?
Are there similarities?

KEYS to remember: 🔑

- Our feelings are pure ***Magnetic Energy***.
- At every moment they are flowing out from us as a ***Vibrational Frequency***.
- How we've been FEELING will affect what kind of Magnetic Vibration we're sending out.
- ***Positive*** thoughts create positive feelings, and positive feelings create positive vibrations, and positive vibrations attract positive situations.
- ***Negative*** thoughts create negative feelings, and negative feelings create negative vibrations, and negative vibrations create negative situations.
- Because thoughts and feelings tend to be ***Habitual***, we may not recognize the positive from the negative.
- Negative vibrations may feel perfectly ***Normal*** to us even to the point of our defending their existence or value.
- Compare your ***Feelings*** to your ***Circumstances* -** what similarities do you see?

*All **attitudes** (vibrations) are **adaptive choices***
*governed by **Learned Behavior** and **Habit,***
AND CAN BE CHANGED!

BUT THE REAL QUESTION IS:

Who am I outside the influence (energy)
of people, things, circumstances and situations ?

Am I just like a "leaf in the wind"?
With no real identity other than what my environment dictates?

The answer is ABSOLUTELY NOT!

****

Why is this important?
Why are we talking about **ENERGY** anyway?
What does this have to do with **ADDICTION**?

WOW!!!

Let's See?

Let's look at POSITIVE and NEGATIVE energy:

We were able to define ***ENERGY*** in relation to another person who we loved being around, or disliked being around.
We agreed that we **Loved** being around Positive Energy, and we **Disliked** being around Negative Energy.

WHY?

Because Positive Energy is NURTURING, and Negative Energy is DEPLETING

As alcoholics and addicts, chances are pretty good that we grew up in environments where there was alcohol or drug abuse, or both. There is also a pretty good chance that our addiction was significantly influenced by our genetics - waiting to be activated with the first drink or drug.

The environment (**energy**) of an addicted family generally includes fear, unpredictability, disorganization, neglect, irresponsibility, dishonesty, and sometimes verbal and physical abuse, and for sure, lots and lots of confusion.

DEPLETING......☹

As children, we had no reference point except to believe that life was scary and that something was dreadfully wrong with "me" and my family.

As children we did our very best to **mask the pain and fear** with **overachieving, rebelling**, or **disappearing** – and everything else in between, to achieve some level of **safety** (false comfort)

Most of all, we had to keep our **"SECRET"**,
or else the **wound** in our family could be **EXPOSED**.

FEAR** was the **MOTIVATOR,** thus, began our **STRESS ...,
We had to learn to lie, pretend, justify, excuse and protect.

As mentioned in the beginning of this chapter, alcoholics and addicts have a special aptitude for reading other people's **ENERGY.**

Now we know why – it has always been a matter of SURVIVAL.

"*This pretense has been with me all of my life. It never goes away, and I don't know who I am apart from it. Because of it, I have never been able to really be OK – just surviving day by day, from one fear to another, from one relapse to another.*" Janice A.

The "Secret" is my Master, I am its "Slave"

Accumulated Negative Energy is **deadly.**

To avoid it, most of us started **drinking/ using** in our teens to early twenties.

We found that in doing so, the **FEAR** was not so powerful. We could **PRETEND** better, and sometimes we even believed we were OK - for a little while.

Still, no one knew the **SECRET,** or so we thought…, because we were **super careful** to hide behind a screen of **NORMALCY.**

UNTIL THE CONSEQUENCES STARTED "SNEAKING UP":

Preoccupation with thoughts of using
Irresponsibility
Failed Relationships
Failing Grades
DUI's
Increasing lies
Using and drinking more
Opportunities lost
Greater FEAR, Less CONFIDENCE
Good friends drifting away, replaced by using friends
Taking advantage of opportunities for easy money to buy substances
Unsafe environments
Family estrangement
Multiple attempts at rehab – always leaving after detox
More and more excuses, justifications, rationalizations, blaming, denying
Careless using
Evictions
Job Losses
Blackouts
IV Substances
Jail

Until one day I woke up -
By God's grace…, I am not sure?
But, I KNOW that I am not this person,
This person is just an imposter.
I am good and free, I am loved and powerful.
I had to go to "Hell" to understand "Heaven".
I had to experience the DARK to understand the LIGHT.
I had to encounter who I AM NOT,
to understand WHO I AM.

But then I forgot…, again, and again. ☹

The ENERGY of "BAGGAGE"

THE BLACK BOX

The **"Baggage"** (fearful memories and actions) that we carry with us from childhood into adulthood, and ultimately to our graves generally falls into **4 basic categories:**

Things that have been done to me by others (make a list)

Things that I have done to others (make a list)

Things that I do not want to remember (make a list)

Secrets (make a list)

This **"Baggage"** steals our joy and constantly saps our energy - like a bad, chronic virus. We go through life continuously trying to "stuff it back into the "Box", but ultimately it comes seeping out at times of **Stress** and **Change**.

We can also ***add*** to the contents of the box anytime by the energy of our own toxic, fear-based thoughts and emotions.

Forgiveness of self and others is always the **KEY**.
Holding ourselves and others **"hostage**" by our refusal to forgive will only continue the suffering.

Our experience of **forgiveness** will miraculously lead to experiences which will result in **gratitude.**

Gratitude and Forgiveness are
the greatest healers. (Gift!☺)

To learn **Forgiveness**, we need someone to **HURT** us.
To learn **Gratitude** we must experience a serious **LOSS**.

Addiction easily provides both!!

With our new understanding of energy, we must further grasp its power for the **LIGHT** and the **DARK.** (Duality)

LIGHT Energy is nurturing.
It is loving, tender and forgiving.
It provides life to humans, animals and plants.
In our most difficult times,
it gives hope for a better tomorrow.

It is the most **POWERFUL ENERGY** on our planet.
When we engage with it, by any positive thought, word or deed,
our entire physiology, meaning **every cell** is aware of it.

For anything to heal, it must have **light**.
Every **light** thought, feeling or emotion
carries its own special **vibratory healing quality.**

℘

DARK Energy is depleting.
It is fearful, controlling and unforgiving.
It provides by contrast, the **stage for the cosmic play of duality.**

It is responsible for our most difficult times, and fools us into believing in our own mortality, failing and separation.

Next to the **LIGHT**, it is the most **powerful energy** on our planet.
When we engage with it, by any negative thought, word or deed,
our entire physiology, meaning **every cell** is aware of it.

DARK ENERGY will suck, steal, confuse and deny our ability to heal.
Every dark thought, feeling or emotion
carries its own special **vibratory depleting quality.**

As alcoholics and addicts with **histories of very dark experiences**,
and **memories of very dark choices and behaviors**,
we habitually think dark thoughts, remember dark experiences,
and expect darkness to prevail. YES??
Yes… ☹

What will happen, by **The Law of Attraction** if we continue to align with the **Dark**?

Well, the fact is that we are actually allergic to **Dark Energy!!**

So allergic that too much of it causes us to **Relapse,** despite the experience of many negative consequences.

Like the **Moth into the Flame,** we can't seem to **RESIST.**

What a **DILEMMA!!!**

As the **Consequences** and **Guilt** continue to pile up again and again, we can't seem to resist thinking, feeling, and believing that:

I am not good enough
I am not smart enough
Nobody understands me
It never works out for me
It's too hard
I'm too tired
I don't trust anybody
Nobody trusts me
I am a loser
I can't keep up
I am a fraud
Everybody knows I will never make it
It's too late
I'm just a fool

EVALUATE THIS ENERGY… What are the Consequences?

DARK Consequences!

But…, putting my **old, habitual**, **negative thinking**, **feeling**, and **believing** aside, the real **truth** is:

I am good enough, I'm ME!!
I am smart in a lot of different ways
I will work hard to help others understand me
I know that God wants me to succeed
It is only too hard if I think that way
I'm hopeful and energized to begin a new way
I must become trustworthy myself
I am a winner when I believe in myself
I can keep up when I keep it simple
I am an authentic recovering addict/alcoholic
I cannot judge myself by the opinions of others
It's NEVER too late
I am just a sweet child of God who has
chosen a very hard path in this lifetime
I WILL SUCCEED, ONE DAY AT A TIME!!
I am not in control – I Surrender to that GREAT POWER that IS!!

Evaluate this energy… What are the Consequences?

LIGHT Consequences!

This is why we cannot afford to align any thought, feeling, or belief with the Dark!

(It will lead us to relapse and create more negative consequences -a very vicious cycle)

*So…, the **Dark** is our **Motivation** to align with the **Light***

The LIGHT IS THE GIFT!!

The Gift of Addiction is becoming the LIGHT!!
(Without Addiction I wouldn't have a CLUE!!)
☺☺☺ (Gift!)

Now that we have a better understanding of what the *Gift of Addiction* is, let's look at

CHOICES & CONSEQUENCES

- Our **"life force"** is that amazing energy that gave us life and continues to work on our behalf despite all obstacles.
- When our choices lead to severe **negative consequences**, our life force may, or may not be strong enough to keep us alive.
- Like any other power source, it must be nurtured and supported by the light to maintain the Body, Mind, and Spirit in optimum working order.
- It is important to understand that consequences for aligning ourselves with dark energy, are **dark depleting consequences** and, consequences for aligning ourselves with light energy, are **light nurturing consequences**.
- This also describes the concept of **Cause** & **Effect**, or **Karma**, the purpose of which is an evaluation of our learning process to ensure the accurate understanding of the lesson, and graduation to the next learning level.
- As our understanding grows, we are able to "see" that there really is order amidst the chaos of our lives.
- There are clues, signals and signposts, subtle as they may be, that can be picked up intuitively, when we learn how to listen. (Gift! ☺)
- Our spiritual path was chosen specifically for our unique needs and purposes.

Next, we are going to learn about the CHAKRAS!

Understanding how these energetic "**power stations**", or "**dynamos**" ultimately govern all life functions will help us understand why "**things have happened as they have.**

Chapter 4

The Chakras

The word **"Chakra"** is Sanskrit for one of 7 principal points of dynamic power, **Energy Centers** in the body that correspond to **Thousands of Nerve Ganglia** branching out from the **Spinal Column**.

These **7 Energy Centers** are located at the base of the spine (tailbone), and **along the spine** at the areas across from the lower abdomen, solar plexus, heart, and throat, then at the forehead, at the point between the eyebrows, and finally at the crown of the head.

The energy from these 7 Chakras regulate all **human processes**, including all **Physical**, **Spiritual**, **Psychological** and **Neurological** systems in the body.

The word **Chakra** literally means **"wheel"** by association with its function as a **Vortex of Spinning Energy** - as an **Invisible Circulatory System**. Each Chakra has its own vibrational frequency, corresponding to the bodily system determining its assigned area of function. It is the adjustment of this invisible circulatory system by your Acupuncturist that improves your "Chi", or in other words, the **quality of your energy** to provide improved health, vitality, and healing.

More information about **ENERGY...**

All of our **states of awareness**, everything that is possible for us to experience physically, mentally, emotionally, and spiritually is associated with one of the 7 Chakras.

When **tension** or **stress** is detected in the associated Chakra, it is energetically transmitted to the corresponding area of the body, thus creating a **symptom**. The symptom serves as a way to communicate through the body that the thought, emotion, or belief is unhealthy and detrimental to the whole being.

Our **state of consciousness** is connected to every cell in our body, and every Chakra associated with those particular cells.
What we think, feel and believe creates our **energy field**, which reflects our state of consciousness.

When our energy (thoughts, emotions, and beliefs) are negative and fear-based, our **symptoms increase**, but when they become more healthy and positive, the symptoms have no further reason for being, and can be **released** according to what we allow **ourselves to believe is possible.**

<u>What we **believe is possible** creates our **reality**</u>

Thus, a **change in consciousness** creates a change in our **energy field**, which must occur before there is a change in the physical body, our circumstances, and our life experience in general.

Some more questions to ponder:

- ♥ Why are some people more affected by germs than others?
- ♥ Why do some hospitalized patients respond to treatment better than others?
- ♥ Why do some people have the ability to recover more quickly from accidents and traumas?
- ♥ Why do habitual relationship problems plague some people?
- ♥ Why do opportunities and "good luck" seem more available to some than others?
- ♥ Why are some people able to respond with trust and faith to seemingly impossible circumstances?
- ♥ Why is forgiveness so difficult for some and easier for others?

Universal Answer:

We create our own reality by the ENERGY we give it.

Bad Energy = Basing our thoughts, emotions, and beliefs on

Fear-Based past, present and future outcomes, creating loss and regret. ("should-have, would-have, could-have")

℘

Good Energy = Listening to our **Inner Guidance** (intuition, conscience) from our own **Higher Power** to think, feel, believe, and make faith-based decisions, reducing tension and stress, resulting in positive outcomes.

So…, which stress creates which symptoms? Let's see???

The first three **Chakras**, are associated with **matter,**
and are more **physical** in nature.

Located at the **Heart Center**,
the **4th Chakra** is in the middle of the seven,
and unites **matter** with **spirit.**

The Heart Chakra serves as a **"bridge"**
between the body, mind, emotions and spirit.

The **Heart Chakra** can be thought of as the ultimate **"Authority".**
(Either my Heart is "In it", or "Not in it")

The last three **Chakras** are associated with **spirit**,
and are more **spiritual** in nature.

When we are able to work through the issues of the first three Chakras,
we can more fully open the Chakras at the

5th -Throat

6th -Spiritual Eye

7th – Thousand-Petaled Lotus or **Higher Power,**
moving us into a **Higher**, **Lighter Vibration** (Energy).

Chapter 5

1st Chakra (Coccygeal, Root)

Location: base of spine (tailbone)

Responsible for the Health of: immune system, skeletal system, bladder, colon, lower extremities *(Do you have physical problems in any of these areas?)*

Represents our FOUNDATION: survival, stability, security, safety, trust

Empowered: Our ability to manage duality, demonstrate courage, trust, endurance, patience, and faith, even under the most challenging circumstances.

Weakened: A history of physical and emotional abuse, abandonment, neglect, unpredictability, chaos, feeling alone, chronic anxiety

Challenge: FEAR (The key factor in the development of symptoms is the **strength** of the fear)

Many of us who grew up in an **Addicted Family** first felt **fear** at an early age. Do you remember how old you were when you first felt fear? This difficult and challenging **energy** formed an unsafe and shaky **foundation** for our early life and development. We felt frightened, alone, angry, inferior, lacking trust, and did not have a "voice" to ask for help. Instead, we created a **"mask"** of normalcy, rebellion, or invisibility. The wall we built around ourselves shielded us from any intimacy with others, fearing that **Self-Disclosure** would **Expose** us to even more **Danger**.

Most of us as adults still carry this **fear**. We have the underlying belief that **life** remains unsafe, we are flawed, we will be abandoned, and there is no real security anywhere. In reality, there was never anything wrong with us. We were born **perfect**, but with the **amnesia** necessary to engage in the **play** (the experience). The play is our **Spiritual Path of Addiction**. To make the play even more challenging, society regards us as **Stupid**, **Lazy**, **Irresponsible, Reckless**, **Foolish, Immoral** and **Insane**, which we are **NOT**, but our **Addictive Behaviors** give society the **Credibility** to define us that way) So..., for us to believe that we are **"Less Than"** and **"Complete Losers"** is totally **Realistic**..., but completely **UNTRUE!**

WHO said this was an **EASY PATH?** ☹ (Remember…, we chose it!)
Not easy… but the **Perfect Path**, for our Soul Growth! (Gift! ☺)

SO, we must understand…

The healthy functioning of our **1st Chakra** is dependent upon our ability to:

- Manage **Duality**. (Light and the Dark)
- Demonstrate **Fearlessness** in the Face of Adversity
- Maintain **Trust** when circumstances breath disaster
- Exhibit **Endurance** when we want to give up

To do this we need an **Unflinching Loyalty and Surrender** to the **God of Our Understanding**

The understanding and the management of the 1st Chakra challenge **(FEAR)** is our **greatest test** on the **Spiritual Path of Addiction.**

Just as the **Foundation** of our house is the most critical to its stability, the healthy functioning of our 1st Chakra is **CRITICAL** to our recovery!

On our Path, we will be back again and again to visit the 1st Chakra

NOTE: There are alcoholics and addicts who **DID NOT grow up in an Addicted Family**, and can trace **no genetic link to ADDICTION in the family lineage**. These folks are **RARE,** but do exist. Our explanation must be one of **TRUST** that the **Soul** and the **Creator of that Soul** had a plan which made **ADDICTION** an appropriate opportunity.

L.G's Story

L.G. is a 46 year old female admitted for medical detoxification from alcohol, Ambien (for sleep) and Xanax and Klonopin (for anxiety). She presented with a history of 3 previous inpatient chemical dependency treatments, typically relapsing within 1-6 months of discharge. She also has a history of obesity, COPD (chronic obstructive pulmonary disease) diabetes, and hypertension. Her liver enzymes are elevated. Vital signs are also elevated: BP 198/90, Pulse 102, Respirations - 26. Height is 5' 5", Weight is 194 lbs. Her color is flushed, skin diaphoretic. She presents as disheveled and tearful, stating, "I can't do this anymore. I am going to lose my daughter and my job." Patient is visibly tremulous, complains of nausea and vomiting over the past 72 hours, and states she has run out of pills, and her last drink was yesterday. She admits to using Xanax, Klonopin, Ambien, and drinking up to a pint of Vodka daily, with the addition of wine on weekends - denies any seizures, but admits to a history of blackouts. She is a single parent of two children, on medical leave from her job as a teacher. Her 21 year old son is in prison for assault with a deadly weapon, as well as the use and distribution of heroin. Her 15 year old daughter is currently staying with her grandmother. The patient has a history of inconsistent follow-up with outpatient treatment and 12-step involvement, but presents today as willing to engage in continuing treatment after detox. She is admitted to the Acute Care Unit for Medical Detoxification, and has agreed to transition to Residential, and then Outpatient treatment as part of her Recovery Plan. Her mother has agreed to keep her granddaughter while Lynn is in treatment, and has also agreed to attend the Family Program to learn more about the "disease" that has plagued their family for generations.

The Psychosocial Assessment reports the patient currently being a third grade teacher in a rural California school district, now on medical leave. The patient relates that she has always been intrigued by the beauty and innocence of children, and has felt most valuable, comfortable and effective in teaching and protecting them from the rigors of the world they will face as adults. She relates that she chose to leave the studies of the higher grades to others who were not as sensitive (fearful) as she is. She further reports childhood memories of an unruly and chaotic home environment where she was "seen but not heard." She recalls how her father instilled this "rule" into her consciousness with his repeated drunken and angry verbal and physical outbursts, while her mother stood by feeling broken and helpless, and her younger brother hid in his room. Lynn began drinking alcohol at the early age of 12. Consuming alcoholic beverages was something that all adults in Lynn's environment did. It was a predominant thread in the fabric of the society she lived in, and her introduction began by sneaking alcohol from her parent's liquor cabinet. She discovered that it made her feel happy, carefree, able to engage in social activities, and be "popular" within her peer group. Her drinking continued throughout high school and college, until in her mid-30's she began to feel "jittery and anxious" without it. With the genetic blueprint of addiction taking its grand place on the tapestry of her life, she was now dependent on alcohol during the day. Without relating her alcohol use to her primary care physician, she sought medical treatment for her anxiety and was prescribed Xanax 0.5 mg. three times a day, as necessary, and Ambien for sleep. Typically, her prescriptions had 2 refills before another medical appointment was necessary. Her physician explained that these appointments were essential for "medication management."

Over the next 10 years, Lynn's drinking increased, as did the dosages of Xanax and Ambien. She soon found that she could not function on her current medication dosages, so "doctor shopping" began in response to her physician's suggestion that her pill use decrease (she still had not shared her alcohol use with her physician) By age 35, Lynn was seeing 3 physicians, purchasing medications from the internet, to include a new benzodiazephine called Klonopin and making frequent trips to local emergency rooms for prescriptions when she ran out. Her alcohol use continued, but was more difficult to manage due to the side effects of nausea, tremors, and blackouts. She preferred using pills to maintain her equilibrium and her "mask" normalcy.

As a strict rule of its priority, substance abuse created many and varied negative consequences in her life. These included failed relationships, medical problems including diabetes, hypertension, obesity and insomnia, as well as job related problems including absenteeism and performance related issues resulting in disciplinary actions. Her relationships with her children also took a "back seat" as her chemical dependency frequently did not permit her to adequately provide for their physical or emotional needs. At age 16, her son was fully engaged in a negative peer group, used drugs daily, and was ultimately expelled from high school for repeatedly coming to school "loaded". It was at this time that Lynn was investigated by CPS (Child Protective Services) for child abuse and neglect. The ensuing investigation resulted in Lynn entering her first chemical dependency treatment program as a requirement necessary to prevent her children from being placed in foster care. Her children went to live with their grandmother while she successfully completed a full treatment course in a local, well-established treatment center. Throughout her treatment, Lynn attended all groups and activities, completed her assignments, and gained a greater understanding of her addictive behaviors.

Finding herself able to express her fears freely, and without judgment gave Lynn a glimpse of peace and serenity, but beneath the surface she harbored a deep and habitual self-loathing which she unconsciously believed never could be removed.

She was able to address some painful memories, but unable to look more deeply into others. Her counselors identified her <u>Resistance</u> and <u>Superficiality</u> as being potential "triggers" for relapse. Upon discharge she followed all treatment recommendations including obtaining a 12-step sponsor, attending 12-step meetings and returning to work. The children were ultimately returned to home under the supervision of CPS. For the next 6 months, all seemed to be going as it should..., she felt physically stronger, she was more comfortable with her life, her friends, family and co-workers seemed to be pleased with her progress - but she had a "gnawing" feeling that this was just temporary. At some level she "knew" that she would return to "using" – her worst fear, and her greatest desire.

Some of us are gifted with an "inner knowing" of who we are, and what we are to do here – however, most of us are not. Taking the opportunity to further explore the idea of ongoing existence after death, we will assume that the concept of reincarnation is an accurate interpretation of the cosmic strategy to provide enough time and experience for each soul to reach maturity – or enlightenment. Many believe that it does not seem plausible that we would experience so many unresolved issues before the show would stop, the curtain would lower, and we would forget it all - never to return for the finale.

As with any grand resolution for the betterment of self, we frequently find ourselves failing to fulfill the requirements for success due to fear and the inability to ask for help. In Lynn's case, her recovery plan was to consistently include 12-step meetings and working with her sponsor. This is where she failed to fulfill the initial requirements for her success in early recovery. Her attendance at 12-step meetings became inconsistent, as did her communication with her sponsor. She knew these activities were important, and she *wanted* to keep up with them, but there were so many other things to do – work, the kids, obligations with friends and family..., just too much on her plate!! Instead of "keeping things simple", Lynn began to obsess over small issues. Rather than reaching out to her sponsor, Lynn rationalized that her sponsor really didn't understand her problems, and it would just be a waste of time talking with her. She further justified her lack of follow-through with recovery commitments by assuming a somatic focus on health issues – allergies, weight gain, frequent headaches, insomnia and such. Not wanting to have to explain her absence at meetings, Lynn chose to not answer calls, and deleted e-mails before she read them. Too much to handle!! Too many demands!!

Though she wanted to be more present for her children, she had trouble focusing on their needs and wants. Work seemed more and more demanding as well..., the constant pressure from parents wanting verbal interactions with her was becoming too much to handle. Her confidence was fading, she was tired and exasperated, the kids were getting out of control, and she couldn't sleep. Ambien...!!!!

As a classic case of pre-relapse, <u>Fear</u> and <u>Anxiety</u> once again, assumed the primary role in Lynn's consciousness, and ultimately took the place of her new found <u>Serenity</u>. Without predictable structure, <u>Anxiety</u>, <u>Fear of the Unknown</u>, <u>Change</u>, and <u>Confusion</u> play havoc with the stability of the addict in early recovery. With all these advantages at its disposal, Addiction typically overwhelms one with its commanding power and control. Thus, relapse becomes "part of the disease" for the majority of addicts and alcoholics. <u>Justification</u> for the use of Ambien was easy for Lynn to explain to her new physician

"I have to sleep!! Nobody can work and take care of kids without sleep!! I have had good results with a medication in the past – I think its name is Ambien." BINGO! Prescription written. Thank you so much!" OFF AND RUNNING!!

Two months later.........., Lynn is on probation at work for absenteeism and parent complaints. To avoid further CPS involvement, her mother has assumed responsibility for her two children because Lynn has become unable to "handle" parenting responsibilities. She is currently using alcohol again, Ambien for sleep, and looking for a new source of Xanax. Recovery is again placed on the "back-burner" of her priority list until the <u>consequences of her use</u> once again take center stage.

<u>QUESTIONS:</u>

What happened to Lynn's relationship with her Higher Power?
Why did Lynn not call her sponsor?
Why did Lynn not get to a meeting?
Why did Lynn not use the recovery "tools" she learned in treatment?
Why did Lynn forget how badly she felt prior to being admitted for detox?
Why did Lynn not remember the CPS experience?
Why did Lynn not remember her children's tears and fears?
Why did Lynn not remember her mother's worry and grief?
Why did Lynn not concern herself with her job, friends, or family?
Why did Lynn not see this act as dangerous and life-threatening?

<u>ANSWERS:</u>

Addiction Is Cunning, Baffling, And Powerful ..., And Progressive.
Addiction Is A Continuing Process Of "Brainwashing".
Addiction Is A Product Of The "Dark Side" Of Duality.
Lynn Lost Her "Connection" with her Higher Power.
Lynn's Wisdom and Common Sense were Overshadowed by Denial.

Through the process of **<u>Denial, Confusion, Rationalizing,</u>** and **<u>Justification,</u>** the **Disease of Addiction** once again caused Lynn to **<u>FORGET</u>** why she couldn't use and drink.

In January of 2014, Lynn was driving under the influence of alcohol, and rear-ended another driver on a California freeway while going 75 miles an hour. Both Lynn and the other driver were seriously injured. **<u>Consequences</u>** for Lynn's "**<u>forgetting</u>**" included hospitalization, incarceration, job loss, bankruptcy, and permanent loss of custody of her children to her mother, as well as heavy emotional "**<u>baggage</u>**" to add to her already overflowing cart.

Lynn's relapse was devastating for her mother and her children, but the family was able to survive due to the new understanding they gained by attending 12-Step support groups for families, loved ones and friends of the addict/ alcoholic, known as **ALANON**. The success of their efforts was primarily due to their ability to **forgive her**, but most importantly, to **forgive themselves** for their self-imposed **blame** and **shame**. The ALANON fellowship, as well as the daily, hourly, and even minute by minute use of the "Serenity Prayer" gave them the antidote for their own "recovery."

***"God, grant me the Serenity to accept the things I cannot change,
the Courage to change the things I can, and the
wisdom to know the difference."***

The Serenity Prayer is the common name for a **prayer** authored by the American theologian Reinhold Niebuhr (1892–1971)

The Serenity Prayer is a traditional element of 12-Step meetings, and has inspired countless addicts and alcoholics to withstand the cravings of their addiction. The Serenity Prayer is a daily prayer, maybe even an hourly prayer in early recovery. Cravings and Temptation lose their Power, Control and Influence in the face of **Serenity**, **Courage**, and **Wisdom.** (Gift! ☺)

The "**Energy Dynamic**" of Serenity, Courage and Wisdom ***and*** Forgiveness practiced and learned in this particular case, by this particular family, will not only provide **"energetic dividends**" to get them through Lynn's drinking crisis, but serve to develop new **Habit Patterns** for future challenges, big and small. (Gift! ☺)

Lynn's mother wrote: *"I was so angry with her for ruining our family. I felt so helpless and guilty for allowing this to happen. I blamed myself for her relapse and the grief of her children. Mothers should be able to prevent such tragedies – I had failed in my most important role, as mother. It felt like I just couldn't go on until one day on my knees, God picked me up and said, "Mary, it's not your fault, your job was not to save her, but to love her. That you did perfectly." I cried and cried and cried until all the tears were gone.* ***I knew that God was guarding and guiding my sweet child. I now have my God, my faith, and my strength to continue loving. I can now forgive her, and myself.***" (Gift!)

Chapter 6

2nd Chakra (Sacral)

Location: sacral spine

Responsible for the Health of: gastrointestinal system, reproductive system, kidneys *(Do you have physical problems in any of these areas?)*

Represents our RELATIONSHIPS: creativity, control Issues, emotions, self-esteem, sexuality

Empowered: nurturing, supportive relationships, flexibility, strength to survive on own, can take risks, stable personal boundaries, can recover from losses/trauma

Weakened: anger, lack of self-control, controlled by others, control of others, manipulation, betrayal, unresolved conflicts, jealousy, secrets

Challenge: GUILT (The key factor in the development of symptoms is the **strength** of the guilt.)

Because we typically do not have a childhood history of a **stable, nurturing** and **predictable environment**, we have looked **outward** in search of those **"light qualities"** necessary for us to grow, thrive and experience a happy life.

We have yearned for **love, acceptance, respect, loyalty, honesty, predictability,** and **unconditional caring** and **concern** from others for as long as we can remember. This may not be a **conscious process**, but our **motivation** has always been to feel **safe** and **valued**. YES?

Because of **FEAR** (1st Chakra), we have questioned whether we could ever **Create** a happy life, or have **Positive Relationships**? And, we were really not sure what one looked like? What about my **secrets**? How much do I share? Which "**mask**" should I wear? Will I be **exposed** as a **fraud**?

All these fear-based feelings and emotions result in the need for **MAJOR CONTROL**! I either assume the identity of **One Who is Controlled**, or **One Who Controls**. If I don't have my "**part**" clear, **I MAY LOSE CONTROL!** And sometimes I DO! **ANGER** is also a **Close Relative to GUILT** in the 2nd Chakra.

But really…, none of these "**Fear-Based Antics**" represent who I am **at all**!

Who I am never had the opportunity to develop naturally. I have always **Controlled,** or have been at the "**Effect of Another Person's Control**", and it has become **Natural** and **Normal** to me - all to prevent the fear of being **EXPOSED** for who I am behind the **MASK**!

QUESTIONS:

How many **Physical Disorders** do I have below the waist?

How many **Failed Relationships** have I had?

How many of these were due to **Control** issues?

How many **Secrets**, **Conflicts**, **Manipulations**, **Lies**, and **Power Struggles** have I experienced in my relationships?

And, how many of these were **Initiated by Me**?.. to feel, once and for all, that I am **Loved and Valued**…, or once and for all, that I am **Not Good Enough** and **Not Worthy**?

Hmmm…?

I am full of **GUILT**

Guilt is very heavy **BAGGAGE ☹!**

(For sure these feelings are a trigger for Relapse!!)

Each one of us at birth "arrives" in a **Family of Origin**, not being given any foresight into who **We** are, or who these **Others** are, or **Why** they are in our lives – or, on our **Stage**.

Only the **Stage Manager** knows the answers to those questions.

As we grow up together, we find that we have an affinity for some, and an aversion for others (duality again!) All the emotions of the 2nd Chakra are "played out" on this **Stage**.

As the **Star of the Show**, we have other **Actors** and **Actresses** on the stage with us assigned to **Major Roles**, **Supporting Roles**, and some playing as **Extras**, coming and going.

Those in **Major Roles** would typically be mother, father, siblings, and grandparents, spouses, children, and best friends.

Supporting Roles are frequently held by aunts, uncles, cousins, and friends.

Those playing **Extra Roles** would typically be friends, bosses, co-workers, neighbors, teachers, acquaintances, and those who "show up" unexpectedly for a specific time and purpose.

(Interestingly, we are also playing on the **Stage of other people's lives** in similar Major, Supporting, or Extra Roles!!)

For example, if we were to assign a **Key Word** for each person playing a **Major Role** on our Stage, it could hypothetically look like this:

Mother: Anxious
Father: Angry
Brother: Supportive
Spouse: Loving
Cousin: Abuser
Grandmother: Protector
Sister: Aloof
Grandfather: Drunk
Daughter: Addict

For the Major Players on our Stage we must ask the question:

What did they come into my life to teach me?
What did I come into their life to teach them?

<u>The Most Important Actor or Actress on our Stage</u>
is the one person who has caused us the **most PAIN in this lifetime**.

This person is responsible for our **Greatest Lesson**, and is ultimately our **Greatest Teacher.**

This person may have been the one who **ABUSED** you, **BETRAYED** you, or **ABANDONED** you – the one who you have never **FORGIVEN**, and the one who has **BROKEN YOUR HEART**.

Through much pain and suffering, we will find that holding him/ her **hostage** by our refusal to **forgive** ultimately increases the **weight of our baggage**, and the **intensity of our suffering**. We may do this for weeks, months, years, or lifetimes.

Through God's Grace,
and our own, sometimes seemingly futile efforts,
we may finally find the **Courage to Forgive**
the **Most Important Actor or Actress on our Stage**,
which was the purpose they held in our lives.

At this point, we will **Miraculously**
experience the **Grace of Gratitude,**
and truly understand that **Gratitude and Forgiveness**
are the Greatest Healers. (Gift! ☺)

The multifaceted, and intricate energy patterns
experienced in our **RELATIONSHIPS**
ultimately **Empower** or **Diminish** our 2nd Chakra.

On our Path, we will be back again and again to visit the 2nd Chakra

B.W.'s Story

I was once told that God creates each individual with specific life threads, and there are one or two life threads that seem to span one's entire life. These special threads are elements of wisdom that each is tested upon and grows from. I have come to discover that two of my threads are patience and connections. This part of my story is on the thread of connections. Healthy life begins with the connections; the trust a babe develops with his parents. Firstborn into a loving home and with extended family regularly around - but trust is a fragile thing.

From the beginning I was one striving for connection. My cousins would watch me when I was very young, and at age three to age seven I was sexually abused by two of them. Although trust broken, this only fed my need for connection. I would follow them around and try to be like them until age ten, only to be teased, ridiculed, even pitied, and seen as more of a tool for cruel amusement than a brother to be accepted. This unhealthy need to find acceptance was reinforced within home as well.

At home when my younger sister was born, expectations were born as well. My father worked long hours and commuted a great distance, so I don't remember much interaction with him during this time, except to enforce consequences of not meeting my mother's expectations. Do not get me wrong, they had a great deal of love for me, but they were young, I was their firstborn, their religion was rigid and appearance was extremely important. From my perspective, while growing up I was praised when I made achievements, but the praise was accompanied with comments of how I could have done better, or sooner, or how I did not do it as my mother would have done. This resulted in hours spent in my room verbally tearing myself down for how stupid I was, how I would never get it right, and how I did not deserve to be alive. You might feel that is kind of a huge jump from receiving looks of disappointment and defeating compliments to the development of my great level of self-loathing. I am not sure how that dark rationale existed, or how it still exists today. I found that since I was "irresponsible", "not meeting my potential", "ignorant", and a "disappointment", that it was easier and better received if I asked for my parents to "rescue" me from the various pitfalls I had created. This varied from projects that would be late, to inappropriate story-telling (8 year olds are not supposed to use profanity or sensual situations in creative reports), to near suspension from multiple detentions, to getting out of manipulating a credit card from a bank as a minor, to preventing an eviction as a young adult, to taking me in multiple times throughout my drug-use when all the money runs out. I learned young that the truth resulted in family being disappointed, but lies kept them happy and the love coming; that is until the truth came out…as it always did. This connection was based on secrets and misguided presentations of love, however my parents taught me about God, how to pray, and that He listens even if He doesn't take away the shame and pain.

I believe it was because of the pain that made it easy for me to be swayed by the first love of my life. She pursued me, broke through my resistance, and doted on me with affection. We were both in college, though I was younger as I had graduated high school early to meet a family expectation. She was different, a rebel with blue hair and a nose ring, and an atheist to boot. She could not be more refreshing from the rigidity I had been experiencing - and suddenly I was free. This relationship, however, did have its similarities. I still lacked self-worth, but it was completely dependent on how I made her feel, which also meant more excitement. Soon we were doing drugs and drinking, but always together - and then came Meth. When Meth was introduced into our relationship everything changed for me, and a new even more powerful relationship began. Again, it was easy for me to give up control just like before, but this love shared none of my values and cared even less for my ambitions. I was able to stay awake for days working, going to school, with a new confidence. I soon began selling these drugs, rising up the ranks, but lost in lies to my family and the girl who was to be the mother of my firstborn. I had no idea who I was and now I had money, friends, and a son on the way. I almost missed his birth as I was attacked with a knife in a drug deal gone bad, but God was there even though I did not recognize it at the time, and I got away with only a cut as a reminder. A deeper cut happened after my son's birth when his mother cheated on me with her ex. I still don't understand my emotions then. I felt as though it was what I deserved, and was to be expected. I yelled, screamed even, only once, perhaps it symbolized my ability to trust leaving my life. I was not angry or resentful, but I could not trust, and I felt empty. I got sober in an effort to clean up for my son. We separated, but a new love had been created through all this pain.

My son was my joy, and I spent all my waking moments with him, but even that was fleeting due to my still lacking a relationship with God or with myself. I moved in with my parents to finish school as suggested by my mother and my son's mother, but it was then that I lost having that close proximity to my son, my daily joy, and then my purpose. I could have finished school and gone back stronger, but I ran into an old love...crystal methamphetamine. It picked up where I left off, except now I had no care for anything. I found myself deep in darkness over the next few years. No regard for myself, having lost that relationship most dear to me, and feeling as though no one cared for me either, I threw myself into the darkness. I engaged in all manner of criminal activity from commercial burglary and grand theft auto, to drug dealing and manufacturing. During this time, I fell for a young woman who also struggled with addiction. I felt I had discovered a connection, as she seemed kind, and had children who I fell head over heels for. I had found my temporary fix to fill the deep void within me, but as with all Band-Aids, they eventually fall off. It was not long before the true nature of this woman surfaced. She was angry, hurt, and scared, which presented in furious rages that included verbal, emotional, and physical attacks. These moments of ferocity were placated by drugs, which became a focus for us both. During these times I would justify dark behavior outside of the home by trying to bring smiles and peace to the little ones within the home. The kids and I would do everything together, the youngest intent on copying me in all things electrical. He would mimic me in words and ways, so I would do my best to be that example, yet still feeling unworthy of his and his sister's love. Those two children were my joy, but one cannot live in both dark and light at the same time, and my unwillingness to commit to surrendering to the light eventually allowed darkness to overcome. Their mother became more and more angry, her temper leading to yelling regularly, destroying things, belittling me, hitting me, and even coming at me fully with a knife only to cut me before realizing what she was doing. During this time I was constantly searching for the one thing to take us back to that time when she was caring and compassionate towards me. That one thing was always eluding me. I became more reckless in my criminal behavior which led to incarceration, and not being there for the children. Ultimately, due to her unsafe behaviors and their biological father's manipulations, the kids were removed from her custody, but another was on the way - my daughter.

It was as if God was giving me a new chance for joy. I now had a new opportunity; I was going to do things right this time, but only as well as an active addict can do. My daughter and I would go everywhere together, see everything a bus could take us to, do everything that the few dollars I had could afford - a lot of story-time at the libraries, ice cream scoops at the Thrifty, and trips to the malls. During this time I made several attempts to stay sober on my own, but only with temporary success. Unfortunately, my past caught up to me again as I found myself guilty of more charges, causing even longer visits to jail. At this point, Child Protective Services became involved, finding a safer and more stable environment for my daughter living with my family, and legally severing my relationship with her. I believe I entered the darkest point of my life as I was now without family, without home, and without love. During my incarceration my daughter's mother slept with another, and although I could not blame her or even be angry for her actions, I was hurt and felt very alone. I found myself without care for personal harm, impulsive, and self-destructive. I ran with others who shared the same darkness, finding myself beat up, cut, and even the target of someone's gun. In the darkness, alone and without remorse, I faced new criminal charges finally sending me to the "Big Time": Prison. I was allowed some time to get my affairs in order before turning myself in, to be locked away. I can only say now that I had no affairs to get into order, but the time allowed me to reach the lowest point of my life, and to be faced with one of my most difficult decisions. I was consumed with the pain and suffering that the darkness of addiction can only provide. I will never forget the night before turning myself in, when I had two needles full of heroin and two needles full of meth. I was planning on using both before going in, but as I prepared the injections, I heard a voice in my head tell me that I would never survive. It was a decision whether to take that next step forward into the dark, or toward the faint glimmer of light still within me. Thank God I chose not to take that potentially fatal step, and assumed my new life as property of the Department of Justice.

I have heard people go to prison to find God; for me I have always believed in God, but regained my connection with Him in that place of desolation. Prison was a place with hatred, violence, and pain; certainly a place for faith to be tested. I still had not committed to an honest life, as I utilized my job outside the gates to smuggle in tobacco - a lucrative means to have what I wanted. I did, however commit to no drinking or drug use. Because of continuing to work in the shadows, the prisoner leading my race demanded that I bring in heroin and meth. His response to my refusal was, "You have 'til next yard to make the right decision". Here it was…, the test. At my bunk I prayed and pleaded with my Father in Heaven. I shared with Him the situation - as if He was just hearing it from me for the first time, and as if He had not been with me the entire time. I did not try and barter selfishly, as I had during past incarcerations. I ended my conversation with Him stating that I knew the decision

He wanted me to make was to decline the demand despite the personal cost to my body or even life.

To this I agreed, but I asked for at least *some* alternative to offer this man. Then unlike any other prayer, I waited for an answer. There I was in the midst of a den where darkness thrived, on my knees in tears awaiting my Father to tell me what to do..., and He did. Outside in the yard it was easy to find the man I needed to talk to as he stood there next to his towering lieutenant, both hands in pockets, holding tools to inflict pain for those who did not follow orders. It appeared to me that I had to cross a perimeter of soldiers to reach the space where he was standing. As I walked toward him, I observed the lack of men who usually surrounded him and where they were located. It didn't enter my mind to change my plans, although I could have abandoned God as per usual, in that moment. Instead my heart and mind cleaved to Him reiterating "I'm yours Father, whatever you wish". That was my moment of Surrender, and after I had relayed the plan provided to me by God, the man still hands in his pockets, and without any visible signs of compassion simply said "Ok, set it up". I went back to my bunk with tears of gratitude, though God was not finished with me in this place. My life was saved, but He wanted me to give up all my shady behaviors. To save my life, the plan God made was for me to show someone else how to accomplish the smuggling of contraband. The guy to replace me was caught, pointed fingers at me, and I found myself locked in solitary for 31 days. I knew why I was there. I continued with my conversation with God, laughing and admitting that the message was received. Admitting to smuggling tobacco made the remaining time in solitary tolerable. Once I was released, I got on a waiting list for addiction treatment. If I had learned anything from attempts to get sober on my own, it was that I could not do this on my own.

After a month without a home, I begin my treatment. I used every opportunity to grow my relationship with God during this time, to get to know Him as family. My own family took a chance and attended some of the celebrations of my achievements in treatment, and I was successful in developing some new life skills, coping skills, and reconnections to God and family. I knew that after I completed treatment I wanted to go back to school, but this would require that I leave the facility. After nine months in treatment my recovery had been born, and having stayed even three months after graduation, I still felt the prompting to go to school and leave on faith – so I did.

I could not return to my family yet, so I started my school program with nothing but what my treatment had provided and what my family felt safe in doing to support me. I had developed new sober relationships who helped me stay strong, saw me as family, and who helped me navigate the school admission process including applying for financial aid. In choosing my career direction, the one profession I did not want to enter was drug and alcohol counseling!! But when the professors stated that I needed to explore the drug and alcohol field, the spirit inside me confirmed my passion. I invested whole-heartedly into this new passion, and at the same time invested in reconnecting with my family. God lovingly provided the opportunities to strengthen my relationships with both my son and daughter. So much gratitude!!

I could not be happier - my connections grew stronger and increased in number. I was given the opportunity to intern at an excellent recovery center where I developed another family as well. I continued in school with the sole desire to serve suffering addicts like myself. Through the 12 Step fellowship of Narcotics Anonymous, I developed a recovery family who I could lean on to help hold me accountable, and to help me address my character flaws and embrace new values. God also blessed me with a beautiful, wonderful partner with whom I share a family of my very own. I now feel blessed far more than I believe I ever deserved, and I have found a new definition for spirituality in my life. To me, spirituality is all about relationships – with God, our family, our community (those we serve and strive to advocate for) and ourselves, past, present and future. To keep my spirituality healthy and strong means a commitment to bring light and growth to those connections. The permanent change in my life all started by my acknowledgement and act of trust towards a relationship with God. At any time in my present life that I find myself struggling with anything, the cause can be linked to self-will, a lack of faith, and attachment to how I believe things should be. The lesson is always Surrender. Through my addiction, I felt the desolation and despair of the dark side of duality, but the God of My Understanding provided the cracks in that darkness for the light to enter. Through that light with God's help, I am able to repair those fault-lines and serve the relationships in my life that have brought me more joy than I could ever have imagined – *"A life beyond my wildest dreams."*

Chapter 7

3rd Chakra (Solar Plexus)

Location: solar plexus

Responsible for the Health of: stomach, gallbladder, liver, pancreas, skin

(Do you have physical problems in any of these areas?)

Represents our: personal energy and power

Empowered: willpower, self-esteem, accountability, self-responsibility, self-confidence, self-control, courage, endurance, honor, integrity

Weakened: inferior, self-conscious, dependent on others, need for approval, poor self-esteem, private agendas, manipulation, demeaning, restless, out of balance

Challenge: SHAME (The key factor in the development of symptoms is the **strength** of the shame.)

With the 1st and 2nd Chakras being responsible for
Physical and **Emotional Survival**, the 3rd Chakra has
the potential for **Manifesting Power** or **Stagnating.**

The way we use the energy of this Chakra is evident in our
ability to CHANGE ourselves, and **CHANGE our situations** in life.

A strong 3rd Chakra represents strong **willpower**, "**sense of self**", and the
ability to transform current circumstances.

It is associated with parts of our consciousness having to do with
Power, **Control**, and **Freedom**,
and also represents our ability to be **at-ease, supportive,**
and **accepting of ourselves and others.**

However, when **weakened** by the **consequences** of **Fear in the 1st Chakra**, and **Control in the 2nd Chakra**, many **Hopes**, **Dreams**, **Plans**, and **Opportunities** are lost due to the priority of managing a scary and unpredictable life**.**

As this **Dysfunctional** process continues, so does the use of drugs and alcohol to **Manage the Stress**, and still appear **Perfectly Normal**, **Functional**, and **Productive**.

Examples of a STRONG 3rd Chakra:
I enrolled in college
I started my own business
I adopted a child
I left an abusive relationship
I got a new job
I joined a support group

Examples of a WEAK 3rd Chakra:
I never finished High School
I lost custody of my children
My business never "took off"
I lost my dream job
I wanted to become a teacher but never did
I have broken many promises to my children

am full of **SHAME**

Shame is very heavy **BAGGAGE** ☹
(For sure..., these feelings are a trigger for Relapse!!)

J.V.'s Story

Throughout my childhood, I never considered that I would ever become the man I am today. I wonder if many of us actually achieve and fulfill the dreams we envision as a child. I certainly didn't, however, I believe my path has taken me exactly where I need to be and has helped me develop incredible power within myself. I am a much stronger person today because of my past experiences, and have learned to embrace my destiny and enjoy life just as it is.

Growing up in a large family of 9, in a small California town where everyone knows everyone, I soon became aware of what others thought of my family's poverty. I was ashamed, embarrassed, felt inferior and started developing low self-esteem. At first I would do all I could to defend my family, but slowly I began disassociating myself from them while becoming more dependent on other people, and on alcohol.

During High School I would stay with friends, party, drink alcohol, and not return home for weeks at a time. While under the influence of alcohol at the young age of 17, I crashed my car into a fire hydrant and received my first DUI. I still maintained my school grades, lettering in band, track, basketball, football and worked summer jobs as a lifeguard. I excelled in football and was awarded a football scholarship to a State University, but the geographical change did not change the insecurities I carried inside me. The fear of not being good enough and not measuring up engulfed me. I dropped out of college and went to work in the Texas oil fields, married a girl from High School and was blessed with two children. All the while my drinking continued.

For 15 years I worked in the oil fields as a welder. I would think nothing of meeting the guys at the bar after work, drinking beer and then driving home. After receiving two more DUI's, I knew I had a problem, and so did my wife - she filed for a divorce. I was sentenced to a year in county jail, but only did 6 months.

When I started back to work I felt ashamed and afraid my employer would find out I was driving on a suspended license. I bought a new house and was trying to put my life back together. I had abstained from drinking for 2 years except a couple of occasions when I drank a shot of whiskey to calm me before I performed in our small band. I was anticipating having my children for the weekend but got a call from my ex-wife telling me that I would have to wait for another weekend. So I decided to throw myself a little housewarming party. I justified my drinking based on something a judge told me at one of my previous court appearances, he said "When I realized I had a drinking problem, I quit. If you are going to drink, stay home." So in my mind, I heard it was OK to drink alcohol at home.

If I would have had the kind of self-awareness I have today, I would have known that I don't stay at home when I drink. I woke up a week later in the hospital.

In my 58 years of life I have made many choices that have led me deep into the darknesses of shame, despair and regret. Of the many significant events in my life none have had a greater impact on who I am today than what happened April, 4th 1995. I don't remember many of the events leading up to, or the actual crash. The estimated impact speed was over 100 mph. It's believed that I pulled onto the freeway, driving north on the southbound Interstate. When I awoke in the hospital after being unconscious for several days I was told of the horrific tragedy I'd caused. My brother told me, "You've done it now! You killed someone." Knowing I'd never be able to forgive myself for all the pain, suffering and death I caused, my Dad also told me, "You'd probably be better off dying too!"

I agreed with him and came so close to dying that the doctors let everyone, including my children say goodbye to me. Surprisingly, I survived to face the penalties of my horrific and deadly choice to drive while under the influence of alcohol. I remember struggling out of bed and into the bathroom with my brother's help to shower. I could not move my arms, several ribs were broken, lacerations were all over my face and body, I had a collapsed lung and a severely bruised heart. The doctor told me most people would die from such injuries. When I looked in the mirror I saw a monster, and I cried not knowing how I would be able to go on living knowing that I had taken an innocent life. During the court proceedings while the district attorney cited all her evidence, I sat dumbfounded and in shock, with my head down and ankles in shackles. I was charged with 2nd degree murder, and the jury found me guilty. My sentence was 15 years to life in prison.

I was, and always will be an alcoholic, but today, with over 22 years of abstinence I have learned an incredible amount about myself, including how to maintain my sobriety on a day to day basis. I remember when others would tell me that I had a problem with alcohol. I just told them to leave me alone because I was not hurting anyone but myself. It took what happened on that horrific night for me to learn that this was never the case. It took me being imprisoned to understand how I not only hurt myself, but I devastated the lives of innocent victims, as well as everyone who ever had anything to do with me.

Feeling lost forever and with no hope, I told my family to just forget about me; to just consider me dead. My mom quickly told me, "No, you cannot do that to your kids." In 1995, I found out my earliest possible parole date would be in 2010. To me that was like a star date that I would never reach. I was told by many in prison that "lifers" never get out, and that I might as well just keep doing what I had been doing, after all, a lot of the prisoners make Pruno and smuggle in drugs. Remembering my horror that someone was dead because I wanted to get drunk, I made a firm resolve to never drink alcohol or use drugs again, whether I spent the rest of my life in prison, or was released someday.

While in prison I did everything I could to find out what was wrong with me; why I did not listen to the warnings, and why I continued drinking despite the repetitive negative consequences. I took every self-help class available and started reading everything I could get my hands on concerning spirituality. I started attending church and 12 Step meetings. I had been so weakened by the consequences of my choices, and felt so much shame and guilt, I knew that I had to take responsibility for my actions. It was time for a transformation of power. It was upon this realization that I had a spiritual awakening after being on my knees for days - crying out to God. I received an overwhelming feeling that I would never have to be alone again. This "feeling" became a "knowing", and helped carry me through all the years in prison, and remains with me today. I also received forgiveness, and in time was able to forgive myself. I was transformed, changed, empowered and freer than I had ever felt in my life, right there inside the gray concrete and steel building, with the razor wire fence.

After serving 18 years in prison, being denied parole twice, earning an AA and then a BA in ministry, I was finally granted parole in June of 2013. Having an undeniable need to finish what I started all those years ago when I dropped out of school because of my lack of self-confidence and need for others approval, I enrolled back in college. I earned an AA in Behavioral and Social Science and then took courses to become a Drug and Alcohol counselor. I desperately wanted to be part of the solution instead of the problem.

Strength from adversity is my driving force. I live my life by this anonymous quote, "Strength doesn't come from what you can do, it comes from overcoming the things you once thought you couldn't do." What I could not do for myself, I now do as a living amends. Not a day goes by that I don't think about the victims of my poor choices, and the pain and suffering caused by my careless actions.

Today, after dealing with my past darknesses, I embrace the light of my destiny.

I tell my story and help others at risk, so that they too may understand the Gift of Addiction.

Connection between Chakras 1, 2, and 3

1st CHAKRA

As an addict or alcoholic, we have been battling with **Fear in the 1st Chakra** (our **Foundation**) for most of our lives, especially if we come from a **Family of Origin** where **Addictive Behaviors** were present and prevalent.

Because of the **Fear** of possible **Exposure** and **Judgment,** we created a false identity of **Normalcy**, **Rebellion**, or **Invisibility (our Mask),** but at all costs, most of us were not willing to acknowledge our pain or ask for help.

Pretense comprised our **Normal Diet**,
and to its defense we still come regularly!

*I am full of **FEAR**.*

2nd CHAKRA

Because of **Fear in the 1st Chakra**, we were unable to engage in **Honest** relationships where we could be **Authentic**, **Flexible** and **Vulnerable.**

Our **Fear** and **Lack of Trust** only left us one avenue – **CONTROL**!
(**Control** of Others, Circumstances, or our Environment **or**
Being Controlled by Others, Situations, or the Environment)

Either **Consciously** or **Unconsciously**, **Fear** continued to be **In Charge**, and we were left "**On Guard**" to **Manage** (Control) the constant **Stress** of maintaining **Balance** on a shaky **Foundation.**

How many failed relationships and relapses were caused by stress??

*I am full of **GUILT**.*

3rd CHAKRA

Because of the **Consequences of Fear** in the 1st Chakra
and **Control** in the 2nd Chakra, my **Hopes, Dreams,**
and **Plans** can no longer be a **Priority.**

Managing the **Fear, Unpredictability** and **Chaos** in my life has taken
precedence over any hoped-for **Accomplishments** I had envisioned for my life.
Instead, I take **The Path of Least Resistance** – in **Survival Mode.**

*I am full of **SHAME***

Anger, **Resentment**, and **Regret**
are frequent visitors to my consciousness,

But, **DENIAL** must be maintained at all costs.
All is well! (Not!)

Chapter 8

4th Chakra (Heart Center)

The "**Bridge** between the lower three **Chakras of MATTER**, and the higher three **Chakras of SPIRIT**

Location: heart, cardiac plexus

Responsible for the Health of: heart, lungs, shoulders, ribs, breasts, circulatory system, respiratory system *(Do you have physical problems in any of these areas?)*

Represents our: love, gratitude, forgiveness, and trust

Empowered: love of Higher Power, love of self, love of others, unconditional forgiveness, gratitude for all life's lessons, feelings of joy and bliss despite difficult situations and circumstances

Weakened: grief, inability to love self, or accept love from others, disconnection from Higher Power, holding on to past resentments/anger, conditional relationships, bitterness, inability to forgive, lack of gratitude, lack of compassion, self-pity, victim consciousness

Challenge: GRIEF (The key factor in the development of symptoms is the **strength** of the grief.)

To describe the **POWER** of an **Open Heart Chakra**, we would have to imagine a **Mother's Love** for her newborn baby wrapped in a cloak of **Joy and Ecstasy,** within the all-encompassing **Tenderness** of our **Great Creator** for all living creatures.

Feelings like **Happiness**, **Delight**, **Bliss** and **Enchantment** are descriptive of an **Open Heart Chakra**, as are emotions like **Adoration**, **Worship**, and **Devotion,** but the greatest of these, is one simple word, **LOVE.**

Love is the **Strongest**, most **Powerful Force** in our universe,
and within **Ourselves.**
The **Heart Chakra** holds within it all **Human Emotions**,
Both **LIGHT** and **DARK,**
Nourishing and **Depleting**

It is our direct connection, route, channel, pathway to our
Great Creator
Higher Power
God of our Understanding

The **Heart Chakra** represents the **BRIDGE** between the **Fear**, and **Shame** of the **Lower Three Chakras** and the **Integrity**, **Wisdom** and **Universal Love** of the **Higher Three Chakras**

Its **Perfect Function** is the **Appreciation** for all the **Lessons** offered by both the **LIGHT** and the **DARK**

Our **Lessons** are responsible for our **CAPACITY TO LOVE** (Gift! ☺)

Within the energy of the **Heart Chakra** is also
Humility, **Gratitude** and **Forgiveness**

LOVE is the **Strongest** aspect of **Light Energy**
FEAR is the **Strongest** aspect of **Dark Energy**

♥The **Heart Chakra** neutralizes this **DUALITY**

Heart Energy is responsible for the
Unconditional Bonds we have with other beings

Heart Energy provides our sense of **Caring** and **Compassion**,
Altruism, and **Generosity**, **Kindness** and **Respect**

Heart Energy carries **Love** as a **Unifying Force**,
the most fundamental part of the universe**,** and our souls

The **Path of ADDICTION**
Requires that we find our **Heart** (Gift!)

♥♥♥

A closed **HEART CHAKRA** says: **"Stay AWAY!!"**
I am unlovable
I am unworthy
I cannot give or receive
I am flawed
I am an imposter
I cannot trust
I am not good enough

But, the disguise I wear is:
Critical of others
Insensitive
Unforgiving
Uncaring
Unemotional
Overly Intellectual
Chronically Negative
Aloof

This **Exterior** conceals a **Broken Heart.**

If we were to visit a **Cardiac Care Unit** and observe the patients admitted there,
we would find many patients with suppressed **Grief**, **Guilt**, and **Regret**,
but most of all lacking the ability to **Forgive** themselves
for the **Anger** they hold in their **Hearts.**

The **Rough Exterior** of our heart provides a **Protective Covering** (mask) needed to carry the **Weight** of the **Baggage** of addiction without being exposed as **Vulnerable, Weak** and **Broken.**

So, we continue, **at all costs**....
to "**Stuff our Feelings**", **Appear Normal**, and **Remain Aloof**,
while **Drinking Alcohol** and/or **Using Chemicals**
to **Mask** our **Broken Hearts**.
(lying, cheating, and stealing, and justifying it all)

Meanwhile, our **Baggage Cart** is overflowing
with the **Heavy Weight** of the contents of
our **"BLACK BOX":**

***Things that have been done to me by others (reference your previous list)**

***Things that I have done to others (reference your previous list)**

***Things that I don't want to remember (reference your previous list)**

***Secrets (reference your previous list)**

~and~

FEAR IS ALIVE in its **Destruction** of our 1st Chakra
GUILT IS ACTIVELY **Controlling** our 2nd Chakra
SHAME IS EFFECTIVELY **Diminishing** our 3rd Chakra

And the **Great God of our Understanding** is lovingly choreographing the unique circumstances which will lead us to our
DARKEST MOMENT.

Our **Darkest Moment** is our **Motivation to Surrender** and ask for help. (Gift! ☺)

At this point, some of us **Fall of the Path** by
Relapse, **Unfortunate Death**, or **Suicide.**

Many of us find ourselves in the arms of those
Loving caregivers who **Understand our Plight**, and
Love Us Enough Not to Leave Us That Way ♥

We may or may not be **"DONE"**
but, we are still **ALIVE** and on the path.

How much more can we take?
How much more can our loved ones take?

We have arrived at the "**BRIDGE" ♥♥♥**

At the **Bridge**" we may resolve to **NEVER AGAIN** use drugs or alcohol.

We have been "**Pulled from the JAWS of DEATH"** (Once again?)

We are beat up
Our livers are shot
We have aged 5, 10, 15, years
These tremors were never this bad before!
What has happened to my memory? (I don't remember...)
Balance while walking is difficult
What is the date?
How did I get here?
DUI? Jail? Really?
Pleeeese!! May I have something for my pain, shaking and craving?

CAN I WALK ACROSS THE BRIDGE?

You say, "Hold on to the Hand of your "Higher Power"
Do I see the SUNLIGHT?
Oh... The Big Book and the 12 Steps!!
I remember those!!! ☺
Meetings?

GREAT!!

Character Flaws?
Cravings?
Triggers?
Amends?

A Sponsor? Phew!! Wonderful..., A GUIDE! ☺
I am WALKING...
Thank you God ☺

Amazing Grace!

(This time it will be different, I don't care how much I have to try, or how long!)

What is on THE BRIDGE?

My HEART?

It Hurts! ☹☹☹

I don't like "**feeling my feelings**"
I am used to **drinking** or **using** them AWAY!

Well..., I'd better keep walking..., **Surrender!**

Gifts On The Bridge ♥

When we are <u>ready</u> to **CHANGE** God gives us:

- ♥ A Teacher/ Teaching
- ♥ Situations/ People who bring out the BEST in us
- ♥ Situations/ People who bring out the WORST in us
- ♥ Afflictions/ Infirmities
- ♥ Sweet Intuitive Messages
- ♥ Scary Tests and Challenges
- ♥ Temptations
- ♥ Unexpected Opportunities
- ♥ Multiple Tasks and Responsibilities
- ♥ Unmistakable Guidance
- ♥ Profound Wisdom
- ♥ Failures
- ♥ Opportunities for Amends
- ♥ Losses
- ♥ Heartbreaks
- ♥ Mind-blowing Insights
- ♥ Incredible Gifts
- ♥ Difficult Confrontations
- ♥ Hilarious Situations
- ♥ Astonishing Miracles
- ♥ The Highest of Expectations
- ♥ Unconditional Love
- ♥ Patience, Trust and Faith
- ♥ An Occasional "Wink"
- ♥ More Tests

"Just hold My hand"...

Sherry Burditt, RN, HN-BC

To **Surrender**, we must **Remember** who is actually in charge of our Lives, our Cause, our Meaning, our Eternity.

Let nothing disturb you,
Let nothing frighten you,
All things are passing;
God never changes;
Patient endurance
Obtains all things;
Who God possess
In nothing is wanting;
God alone suffices.

Saint Teresa of Avila - (Lines written in her breviary)

****

L.M.'s Story

The journey to my heart has been filled with love, laughter, heartbreak, lessons, hurt, anger, and experiences that continue to shape me. I was only truly aware of this path 10 years ago when I had to lose what felt like everything, in order to come to the realization that I would gain the most important piece of my heart, God.

I was born as the first child to loving parents, who eventually had three more daughters. My childhood memories of family vacations, holidays, family, and friends still fill my heart and have created the mother I am today. I attended Catholic school for the first six years of my life, although I never understood the reason, except that it was for a "better education". I learned about God, we went to church twice a year, and that seemed normal. I was grateful however that my parents allowed me to attend public school in middle and high school. In these years, I learned the value of friendship, I fell "in love", and I began discovering who I was (or so I thought). I received average grades during school, never fully putting forth my best effort. My interests were spending time with friends where I felt accepted, and more honestly, where I could escape from the secrets in my home.

I was 14, I was mostly happy, carefree, and had a life that my friends seemed to want. My house was the escape for many of my friends who were struggling with their own family secrets. These "unspoken secrets" bound us together and connected us in a way that we each needed and wanted, but without any of us really being aware. I treasure these friends still, 30 years later, because without them, it may have been unbearable. My parents did their best providing, loving, and making us feel important, but deep down, something told me they were struggling.

I must have been about 14 the night my life began to unravel. Not really understanding what was going on, I was told my sister tried to hurt herself. I felt scared, lost, angry, but most of all, disconnected. I no longer understood my relationship with her, and instead, became resentful that I had to go to therapy. It hurt my heart to see her so broken, to see her struggle, and to witness the thread that tied our family together, unravel. It happened so quickly, and in a blink of an eye, everything changed. After this incident, my sister became rebellious, and with that, I found my place with her again. We had a large group of friends, so it didn't matter the years that separated us. We partied, snuck out of the house, and partied more. I specifically remember drinking the vodka in my parent's fridge, wondering what it would be like, what it would taste like. I replaced the vodka with water, and from that moment on, drinking became a part of my weekend adventures with friends. It never occurred to me that alcohol may have been part of my escape; to me, it was simply what teenagers did to have fun!

High school years seemed never ending, but in a good way. I went to football games, spent time with friends, fell in love, went to dances, partied, meanwhile spending less and less time with my family. That is what teens do, right?! I found where I belonged; I was connected. Home life was still strained; fighting and yelling ensued, but it began to feel sadly normal. The love that was so freely expressed came to a shattering close. No longer did I hear, "Goodnight Mom, I love you." "Goodnight Dad, I love you." "Goodnight sisters, I love you", with their responses filling the nighttime air. Instead I heard the whispers of the Dark threatening our once Light-filled house..., more secrets.

I remember it so clearly, Christmas with just the five of us, not six. My sister was in rehab once again for her addiction to meth. My parents seemed so sad, although putting on a brave happy face for the rest of us. I also felt a sadness, but deep down, was relieved that this year may be different. I wouldn't have to walk on egg shells, or say mean things in return to her comments. Christmas ended in peace, however the roads ahead were bumpy, dark, and scary. I knew little about the disease of addiction, but what I did know is that my life had completely changed because of it. I wasn't allowed to talk about it with anyone, I wasn't allowed to upset my sister because she may run away again, I was to create the peace, to be strong, and to protect my little sister.

I was lied to, stolen from, and physically and emotionally hurt by her. I was angry, bitter, and resentful because this was not how it was all supposed to go! But life did go on. I continued down my path, graduated high school, went to college, graduated again, fell in love, got my first full-time job, got married and had kids. Whew! This is how life is supposed to be, I was back on track! I was enjoying life, meeting new friends, going on vacation, growing in my career, and thriving. I was now free from the dysfunction in my family, and could separate myself from the addiction that still threatened our bond. I could remain close to my family from a distance. I could visit with my family, but return to my home. It all seemed perfect, until it was not.

I became lost, and while I imagine that it happened over time, again it felt like it was in an instant, and everything changed. I felt like a stranger in my own home. I shopped and worked out as much as possible in order to escape these horrible, dark feelings. I was scared, ashamed, and triggered by painful memories of disconnection. New secrets developed and rocked the very foundation that I had worked so hard to create. My husband and I both made choices that forever changed our relationship. Therapy became a place I could finally open up about my past secrets, long time anger, resentments, and grief over the disconnection from my heart, from love. I swore to myself I would never stop saying "I love you" to those that matter. But I did. My heart was walled up, although I saved the little that remained for my children. I had nothing left for me or anyone else. I wore a layer of masks that protected my secrets, my shame, and my unresolved hurts. But the jig was up…, I couldn't do it anymore. My brokenness and feeling disconnected was unbearable, it was all too familiar, in a sense. I wanted out! I didn't know how to talk about it except in therapy. I was too scared to reach out to family and friends. It felt dark, bleak, and hopeless. I wanted out! I found myself on the floor of my bathroom, a wife, a mom, a successful (or so I thought) adult, wanting to end my life. These moments on the bathroom floor, curled up, crying and trying to think of what would be the quickest way to shut out the pain, felt like forever. I was ashamed that I would even entertain these thoughts because it would hurt the ones that loved me. In those dark hours, I heard a faint whisper, I listened, nothing. I grew quiet. The thoughts stopped for a minute. I heard the whisper again. I listened. It was me saying, “God please help me.” Through my muffled cries, the statement repeated itself over and over. I woke up in the morning. It was a new day. I looked in the mirror and the tears came flooding. I immediately went to my kids and loved them with more gratitude than I had in many years.

The moments from this point on were excruciating. Addiction finally won and took my sister off this earth, and my marriage ended. Where was God???? I was in a fog - daily life felt like a blur. All I remember is putting one foot in front of the other. I would tell myself, “You can do this - you just have to go to work and be a mom”. But could I?? I trudged along, crying and screaming inside - but more whispers came. I fully disconnected from what seemed like everyone and everything. Little did I know was that God’s grace and love for me kept me connected just enough to reach out to the few I trusted, and He seemed to be one of “them”. Therapy that I once despised became my lifesaver. Days got easier, but the hole in my heart remained, and was still closely protected by my walls. I heard the faint whisper again, I listened, really listened. This time it was from God and he was saying, “Get up, your life isn’t over.” I kept whispering and so did He.

I didn’t know if I could believe him. I was still embarrassed that I could not hold my marriage together, and in the midst, managed to push away all of my friends. I felt I had nothing but my family, kids, and work. But really, I had God, my kids, family, people who cared for me, and the purpose that God put me on this earth to fulfill. Everyone was perfectly placed on my stage of this production called LIFE. I found an angel in my life who has taught me so much about my path. I learned that all of my experiences have been perfectly orchestrated so that I may be free to be a loving, compassionate, strong, courageous, independent, purpose-driven warrior, but mostly, God’s loving servant who I was always meant to be. She has, and continues to teach me so much about my gifts, life, love, forgiveness, and most importantly, God. This beautiful connection has allowed me to believe in myself once again through my relationship with God.

Today, I can honestly say that this path has not been easy. Sometimes, I doubt if I am on the right path. And I can also honestly say that I still struggle with allowing myself to be vulnerable to all of the challenges and obstacles that God has intended for me. **But what I do know is this**..., I have discovered so many gifts through all the pain, and God was there for me every moment, and continues to be. **The gifts I have received represent a new understanding** that I am a loving child of God, I am smart and have a passion to continue growing and learning, I am an amazing mom who dedicates my life to my children, I am worthy to receive and give love through God's eyes, my family loves me for who I am, I am grateful, I am open, I am courageous, I am teachable, I am capable, I am able to forgive myself and others, I am able to find love again, I make a difference, I am able to remove my walls that I so carefully built, I am an inspiration to others, I have a special gift of helping those who struggle with their brokenness to find their journey back to their hearts. None of this would be possible without God. My heart is open and full of gratitude. Thank you, God.

Chapter 9

5th Chakra (Throat)

<u>Location</u>: Throat

<u>Responsible for the Health of</u>: throat, thyroid, neck, vertebrae, mouth, teeth, gums

(Do you have physical problems in any of these areas?)

<u>Represents our COMMUNICATION</u>: choices, honesty, self-will, self-expression, integrity

<u>Empowered</u>: honest, personal authority, accountable, self-disciplined, authentic

<u>Weakened</u>: co-dependency, inability to define own needs and wants, or make decisions, lack of will power and authority, fear of assertion, inability to speak own truth, exaggerating or altering the truth, gossiping, multiple addictions, victim consciousness

<u>Challenge</u>: DISHONESTY (The key factor in the development of symptoms is the **strength** of the dishonesty.)

As with all the Chakras, optimal functioning of the 5th Chakra is dependent upon a having a strong FOUNDATION, or 1st Chakra.

As we move into higher spiritual frequencies (above the waist)
we are challenged to identify, maintain, and apply
our lessons of **Faith** and **Surrender** (1st Chakra),
our **Self-control** (2nd Chakra), our **Courage** (3rd Chakra),
and **Gratitude** (4th Chakra), so that when we are faced with
having to **assert** ourselves, **express** our needs,
or make important **decisions,**
we will be able to rely on our own
Foundation of Integrity
(thinking, feeling, speaking
at the right time, for the right reason) Gift! ☺

The main challenge of the 5th Chakra is Doubt and Negative thinking, which can result in Dishonest, Inauthentic Expression, and Choices.

The energy of **Dishonesty** is dark and heavy, with its origin being **Fear in the 1st Chakra**, and ultimately affects our **Personal Integrity**, and all the Chakras below it.

☺ **Authentic Expression** is not something that comes easily ☺

There's a delicate balance between
saying what you mean and **being hurtful or critical**.
However, **holding onto something** that **needs to be expressed** for **FEAR** of hurting someone else's feelings, being misunderstood, denied, criticized, or judged

CLOSES OUR HEART
STEALS OUR POWER
DIMINISHES OUR INTEGRITY

TIP: If what we are saying or not saying, doing or not doing is based on **FEAR**, then we know that we are out of **INTEGRITY**.

* The healthy functioning of the **5th Chakra** is the **test** of all Chakras below it.*

When we are not struggling with
Fear in the 1st,
Guilt in the 2nd,
Shame in the 3rd,
Grief in the 4th,
or, any other dark energy,
our **choices** and **expressions**
can be truthful, authentic, and loving.

KEY: *Our COMMUNICATION with the*
God of our Understanding *will provide the* ***guidance***
necessary to make ***authentic*** *decisions and choices*

A.S.'s Story

To understand my story, I must begin with my childhood where the pain began and the secrets grew. My mother and father were already well into their addiction when I was born. My father was an alcoholic/drug addict and my mother an overeater and perpetual victim. I have three sisters, two older and one younger. My father, a Vietnam vet was an angry unhappy soul who took his frustrations out on his wife and his four daughters. I grew up very fearful of my father and tried to be invisible. My father firmly believed in "spare the rod, spoil the child", however his idea of the rod or discipline not only included his belt or a cord up and down the back side, it also included being locked in closets and attics with threats of ghosts "taking care" of us for him. We were tied to our beds multiple times so he could pass out for hours without disruption. My father's use ended when I was seven years old, however the abuse continued into puberty. I was eleven years old when I first tried smoking marijuana and crystal meth. I was hooked immediately and was on a fast paced spiral downward. At thirteen years old the memories of my childhood flooded my mind and I became suicidal. Numb and lost, my parents sought help for me from family counselors, resulting in my first rehabilitation experience. I completed the program after one year, but it did not take long for me to find myself back out in the streets again searching for that one thing that would fill the emptiness. Because I was so young and did not have the means to earn money, I resorted to the only thing I had, my body, to get the drugs I craved. Sex became a tool for me to get what I wanted, and I used it to the fullest extent. The men did not care that I was only fourteen and fifteen years old. During my teenage years, I returned to the same rehabilitation center two more times, however the final time I was totally resistant and fought the whole time. I told my father that I wished for him a slow painful death, and was happy he was HIV positive.

All through high school I continued my drug use and was introduced to the local gangs in the area. I was not initiated into the gang, but as a female, I was able to become affiliated through giving my body to multiple members. This lifestyle reinforced the code of secrecy, never saying anything about anyone, or who did what. As my gang quickly became my family, I ran away from home, dropped out of school, and engaged in the life of a "gangbanger". Many times to eat or get drugs, I strong-armed unsuspecting innocent adults or children.

My father's health was failing due to his secret life as a gay man, who found love by soliciting men. He soon contracted the HIV virus, but it was not until five years after his death that my mother let his "secret" out.

After having two children with two different men, I found myself left alone again, lost with absolutely no self-esteem. I soon met another man who I believed was the answer to all my prayers. I was immediately addicted to him. He controlled everything I did, including how I was to talk and dress. I feared him more than I feared my father, but a good girl does not tell anyone about the man in control. He never hit me, but the threats of violence against me and my family were enough. I believed him when he told me he would kill me. When I started looking into schools to better my life, he easily talked me out of it; after all I was stupid, uneducated, and had nothing going for me. Under the influence of this controlling man I committed a violent offense. We somehow were able to get away with it twice. Eventually, he was caught and I made the decision to turn myself in to the police. It was in that moment that I made the decision to speak out and take control of my life. I made the choice that changed my life forever.

For those violent offenses, I was sentenced to twenty-seven months in a federal penitentiary. During that time, God changed my heart. I grew up and began to accept that I am an addict, and that I desperately needed to surrender my life to a "Power Greater than Myself". While in prison, I found the God of my Understanding. I literally fell to my knees and prayed for an understanding of His will in my life. His answer to me was that He had literally "removed me from my life" to open my eyes to the pain I was responsible for. He showed me that I needed to make serious changes, or my future would be nothing more than the present situation I found myself in - prison. God gave me the choice of continuing down the destructive path I was walking, or facing my past and reconciling it; accepting it for my truth, not something I could change; only something I could accept and learn from. With God's help, I finally found my voice and was no longer willing to allow my past to define who I was; God would have control. In prison, I took every available class from parenting, to a year-long drug and alcohol course that would offer reduced sentences for individuals; however I was not eligible for the sentence reduction. But for me, I took these courses because I knew I would need all the help I could get to overcome my pain, and to battle my addiction. I knew it would not be an easy path, and that there were many lessons God would teach me along the way. After being released from prison,

I was indescribably overwhelmed with responsibility, fear of failure, and a large debt to the government, and after much deliberation, I made the decision that suicide was the only answer. I am not sure if I had any specific plans, I only knew I did not want my children to be the ones to find me; it would have to be outside of the home. I just could not imagine being any good to anyone; I could not see the path God had planned for me. However, through the next five years, God once again changed my heart, changed my life, and opened my eyes to the possibility life had for me. It was no longer about me; I had a larger destiny ahead of me. God helped me to see that the suffering I endured was so that I could help others with true empathy; to help guide others to God's light. My voice and my truth were God's tools to give light to the darkness. I began taking college courses to become an alcohol and drug counselor. At the same time, I was in court ordered therapy and started opening up and purging the darkness from my broken soul. The light of truth began filling up the cracks of my brokenness, and life became my only option - a life filled with speaking my truth, and loving the hurt souls God saw fit to place in my path.

I am now blessed in so many ways. My children received the mother they always deserved, one who put their needs before hers and was involved in every aspect of their lives. Today, they are both grown up, married, and have each given me a grandchild. My grandchildren won't see their grandmother drunk or high; they will not know what it is like to live in fear, and not know how to openly and honestly communicate with their family. My children and I are now able to have an open relationship where communication is the most important aspect of our bond. I have never held the truth from them and they have been willing and able to share their fears, thoughts, and concerns with me - God being present in all our affairs. Recovery has taught me that my relationship with my Higher Power, and placing my sobriety as priority is the only way I can live with happiness and integrity. Addiction has been a long hard path, however the connection I have with my Higher Power and the freedom of owning my truth, and having a voice to share my experience, strength, and hope is the greatest gift I could have ever imagined. It keeps me forever moving toward the light.

Chapter 10

6th Chakra (Spiritual Eye)

Location: point between the eyebrows

Responsible for the Health of: brain, eyes, ears, nose, pineal and pituitary glands, central nervous system *(Do you have physical problems in any of these areas?)*

Represents our WISDOM: intelligence, reasoning, intuition, insight, imagination, clarity, awareness, "knowing"

Empowered: insight into self and others, intuitive, emotional intelligence, inspiration to others, able to receive and follow divine guidance, "6th sense", strong conscience, can "see" others, can "sense" outcomes

Weakened: disconnected from the Heart (4th Chakra), overly logical, intellectual and rational, "closed mind", disconnected from inner intelligence ("knowing"), detached from emotions of self and others, fear of change

Challenge: ILLUSION (The key factor in the development of symptoms is the **strength** of the illusion.)

The '**Spiritual Eye Chakra**" allows us access to **Inner Guidance**, and direct connection to **Truth** through **Meditation**.

The Spiritual Eye, is located at the **point between the eyebrows**, and is the connection between our **body** and our **spirit**;
between the **material world** and the **spiritual realms**.

When we connect with **6th Chakra energy** through **Meditation**, we are capable of conquering any obstacle by tapping into our **Inner Wisdom**, and the **Direct Guidance** from our Higher Power.

Our meditation area should include the following:

A **Location** separate from other energies (even a small closet, or corner of a room)

A **Meditation Seat** – A cushion (if sitting in lotus posture), or a straight-backed chair

An **Altar** of your choice - Any special pictures, objects, flowers or candles.

Meditation Posture – spine straight, feet flat on the floor, eyes closed with gentle gaze focused at the point between the eyebrows (Spiritual eye), chin parallel to the floor, hands with palms upturned, resting at the junction of the thighs and abdomen. Be relaxed but alert.

Our goal is that once the meditation posture has been established, no further movement occurs.

Beginning our meditation practice with a **Prayer** helps establish our **Intent** to **Connect** with our **Higher Power.**

MANTRA - At the beginning of meditation, the use of a Mantra is beneficial in **setting our intention** to aid our **focus** and **concentration**.

A Mantra has **powerful vibrational energy** which can raise our consciousness to a **Divine frequency** with committed practice (Gift! ☺)

Our Mantra can be as simple as:
"Let go, Let God", "I want to feel Your Presence", "My God", or "I love You."
The words are mentally spoken in **rhythm** with our **inhale** and **exhale**, while maintaining our **focused gaze** and **meditation posture**.

The purpose of a Mantra is to **Quiet the Mind** in preparation for "**Talking to God**", and "**Listening Intuitively** for **God's Response**". The **Energy** of the words of the Mantra, and our **Intention**, can also direct **healing energy** to any part of the body.

FOCUSED (Eye) GAZE:

With deep concentration, and the gaze gently

focused at the point between the eyebrows,

we will see the **exquisitely beautiful Divine light**

behind our closed eyes, a **"Gift"** which is worth

all the challenges and tests of our Path,

reminding us that we are connected, and have always

been connected to the **Great God of our Understanding**.

♥

How Meditation Can Support Your Recovery
...allowing your Recovery to take root and blossom

- The **Inner Quiet** established in meditation will create our own **Inner "safe place**," a calm center we can feel in our Body, Mind, and Soul - a spiritual place to go when outer situations feel stressful or confusing.

- Meditation will give us **Deep Neurological Healing** that will allow our body to relax completely. This peace and healing then will spread into our mind and heart - making it easier to access **Inner Guidance.**

- Neither our **Intellec**t nor our **Will** can take us to this Inner **Calm Center of Love, Joy, and Peace**. Meditation can, because in meditation we **Surrender** our egos and *allow God to draw us to Him.*

- By concentration at the **Spiritual Eye**, when our thoughts and emotions subside, we transfer our consciousness from the Mind/ Body to the Soul, and move from **Restlessness** to **Peace**.

- In meditation we can rise above the body's aches, pains, and constant need for attention. Over time we come to experience oneself as Spirit, capable of so much more than we ever thought humanly possible. The Spiritual Eye is the **"microphone portal"** through which we can talk to God directly. His response will intuited at the **Spiritual Eye**, and felt in the **Heart Chakra**.

• Ways to Deepen Your Mediation and Inner Life

- Be balanced. Eat a healthy diet with lots of raw vegetables and fruits. Do not become sleep deprived. Exercise daily. Spend time in nature. Keep life simple. Establish "An Attitude of Gratitude".

- Strive to create friendships based on honesty and true affection. Look for those people who express the positive side of a negative psychological habit you wish to eliminate from your nature. (Ex: If you are basically fearful in nature, strive to be around those who are calmly confident and fearless.)

- Be aware of what you choose as your mental nutritional diet. Choose wisely those TV programs, CD's, and books that are encouraging and healing, that soothe your nervous system, not shock or excite it.

- During the day, remember to think of and talk to God often –Most important! What we do during the day will affect our meditation at night.

♥

The Value of Developing a Daily Meditation Routine

- As we make morning and evening practice of Mediation a priority, we are actually shedding our **fear-based** consciousness, and moving into the **higher** vibratory levels of **Love, Joy,** and **Gratitude** – (Purification!) Gift!

- As we consciously work to raise our vibration, we cannot afford to re-engage with any **dark** or **negative** thought, feeling, belief or action.

- Our consistent meditation practice must become a priority - **every morning** upon awakening, and **every evening** before bedtime, beginning with 15 minutes, up to 1 hour, or more, at least once a week.

A word about "Gifts" at this level..., with continued practice,

We will be better able to accept **Duality** without losing our **Foundation.** (1st Chakra)

Our **Attachment** to outcomes will lose its stronghold on us. (2nd Chakra)

Our **Personal Power** will return and expand. (3rd Chakra)

We will see our world with greater **Love** and **Compassion** (4th Chakra)

Our **Communication** will demonstrate greater **Integrity** (5th Chakra)

We will notice frequent **Synchronistic occurrences**, and **Opportunities** (6th Chakra)

♥ These are the exact things we were seeking in our use of drugs and alcohol. Now they are legitimately ours!! Gift!! ☺

K.D.'s Story

My story begins as a Godless one. It's a story with the death of child at the hands of addiction. No, actually, that isn't my story - that is the story of my mother and my father but it was the beginning of mine and almost became mine. That said, I presume that is why there was no God in mine. I was raised to believe in science, knowledge, intellect and man. I was raised to believe that we were our own creators, nothing was beyond reach and there was a logical answer to everything. I was raised in books and denied the discussion of spiritual things. I was taught that good acts were innate and that everything was explainable.

I grew up with my nose in a book and on the outside my world looked perfect - I thought it was. I had a "happy" family, we saw a lot and I was taught a lot. We were always busy learning, traveling, exploring, and adventuring. I was sheltered. We had no TV in our house and I commuted an hour each day back and forth to school and went away every summer. My life complete in so many ways, lacked two things, a spiritual understanding, and people. My addiction ended teaching me about both. When your nose is in a book you don't have much room for friends. I never really learned how to play or bond, but none the less I remember my childhood as bright.

As I stated, there was no room for God in my house. It was pounded into me that God was only for the ignorant, something to make things ok for people when really it wasn't. God was only for the weak minded. In spite of this, when I look back, I remember moments of inexplicable joy. Such as looking at a field or at a mountain, smiling so broadly that my cheeks would hurt and tears would fill my eyes for no apparent reason; or reading a creative metaphor in a book and feeling my heart jump into my throat just because of the beauty in the line. I didn't know it at the time but this was my Higher Power whispering at me. When I was around 6 I experienced one such moment.

My family and I were driving across the country at night and I was lying in the far back seat of our van with one of those painful smiles stretched across my face. I was gazing out the window at the stars and the plains as we zoomed across Idaho or some such place and tears began to roll down my face. I said to myself, "I know the thing that all the adults have forgotten," I peered over the seat at my parents who were oblivious to the miracle happening right behind them, and I'm never going to forget!"

In that moment, I experienced the most intense joy of my entire life. Why is this important? It's important because every year I would check in with myself. I would question "Do you remember?" and I would!!! Such Joy!! I remembered! I continued to grow and continued to remember!! I would hold it close to my heart and the smile would reclaim its place across my face. All the while I was filling myself up with information and knowledge; I took great pride in the vastness of my intellect for just a young girl. And as my knowledge grew so did my ego. And the larger my ego grew the smaller my secret shrunk. The world and the information, in time outgrew my secret all together and one day, as I entered my teens I remember doing my normal check in and being surprised and deeply saddened that I had forgotten, just like all the other adults around me. At this time I became fully immersed in the world of man. I hadn't known it at the time but what I knew as a child was how to see the world through Gods eyes. It took a deep and sad journey through darkness of addiction to find my way back to the light in that child, but without it I never would have begun to remember again.

Back to the story…My ego was running rampant. I constantly compared myself to everyone and obviously put myself above them. My supposed "intellect" disconnected me from the heart. I always had a way of seeing or saying things that were perceived as "weird" or different, and when I started using drugs I would justify it as opening me up to "see" more. All of my heroes were authors and artists, and had all suffered from addiction. Their stories and the way they saw the world pulled at my heart strings - I craved the insight they had, so I jumped in!!! I would rationalize my drug use as a means to an end; that I was doing "research" towards a deeper understanding. I wanted to see the whole world; not just the beautiful places. I wanted to know all the feelings, I wanted to dance all the dances, and sing all the songs. I have always had an addiction to more. When I look back on my "use", I am now able to see that there was truth in my rationalizing, there was merit in my journey, My Higher Power knew what I needed, and I guess I did to. I was granted a road of suffering, but was one of the fortunate ones who made it out alive. I believe it was for the purpose of reconnecting my heart and my mind, and clearing the clouds that blurred my vision.

Along my path I saw some of the most gorgeous souls trapped in brown paper boxes, covered in dirt, with no teeth left in their heads. I met the ones the world had forgotten, or tried to deny ever existed at all. With each one, I was privileged to get to know the childhood joy of my secret, and it would reinvigorate me. I wanted to get lost with them, and for a while I did; the rag pickers, the beautiful losers living under the bridge. The more I walked with them the more lost I would get. I would have stayed stuck, but at some point I realized I also wanted to live.

During my time filled with every drug known to man, I suffered many losses including custody of my child. I was raped, I was beaten, I was robbed, I begged and sold myself for pennies, and completely forgot how to live. I was homeless, I was jailed, I was institutionalized and hospitalized. I was completely surrounded by darkness. The light I had yearned to see in others became overtaken with nothing but darkness. They say we have to see what we are not in order to see what we are. At this time I also realized I had a gift (the gift of my addiction). I was able to see that sadness in others that they tried to pretend didn't exist. This gift became my strength, it felt like my sort of "super power" in an unforgiving world. But I misused it to manipulate and hurt others. It was all I could see. I could pick it out of you, and grind it between my teeth. I had lost my ability to see any light in anything, there was only darkness.

All along this path I held onto that notion that there was no God, there was nothing spiritual in nature going on because that wasn't real. It was a laughable joke to me. Today it seems funny that I was so certain. But along the path bits and pieces fell in to place, and in spite of all the darkness and chaos around me, I was given glimpses and signs.

My use had started young with alcohol at probably 13 years old. I should say alcohol and young boys - they seemed to go together. The first time I drank it was a black out. I remember throwing up all over myself but I also remember that I felt included. I had never felt included before. The summer after my sophomore year of high school I went away for the summer and stayed with my grandparents for holiday. They had a beautiful house on a lake and they trusted me. I got a job at a country club and began partying. I was a virgin, and basically naive. That summer I was raped and my offender bragged about it after, at a party. I was so ashamed and felt so dirty.

I wanted my power back. I, then proceeded to sleep with 18 men over two weeks-time, and drank to a black out every night. I was 15 years old. The light became dimmer. This was the summer my perceptions and life began to really change.

I had gone back to school after that summer of ruckus, and life resumed as normal. I continued to be my exuberant self, didn't have sex for a year, and only drank occasionally on the weekends, but I continued to feel separated from others and different. I always had difficulty making meaningful relationships, and still have to push myself today. For the next couple of years I was a weekend /summer time drinker. I thought it was normal. My mother, who had been sober throughout my childhood, had relapsed some time back. It was a common occurrence for me to find her passed out with a bottle of wine or pills. When I had my period I was given a Vicodin, and when I was stressed about school I was handed a half a Xanax. No big deal. That was what people do, right? My mom had a great job, was successful, owned her own home, and took lavish vacations; there couldn't be a problem. My mom has since lost not only the house, and the cars and the jobs, but her life to this disease. But, returning to my story - my access to alcohol, and the acceptance of drinking in my household made it possible for me to get the one thing I had always wanted, but had not known how to get, friends!!! My use remained limited to drinking and I continued to thrive in school. It became the cornerstone of my ego and pride - my mask to the world that I was ok, when internally I felt completely disconnected from others, as an island.

My social group had moved onto smoking weed but it took me a year or two to catch up to them. Then one day that changed too. I had turned in a paper for an English class, one of my girlfriends had as well. I had slaved over this assignment and took great pride in the work I was turning in. I had also edited my friend's paper and knew that hers had been written as if by a child. My ego was soaring when I compared the two. We received our papers back and right on top in a big bold red ink we both had received A's. What?!?!!!!! I was so confused. I confronted my teacher in a fury and I was given the same reply I had received several times throughout my childhood. "Honey, we expect more from some people than others and grade based on abilities.

I was defeated. That day I started smoking marijuana. Within a week I was snorting cocaine on a daily basis. I had decided that the effort I was putting in wasn't worth anything anyway. My mask changed. I was no longer the overachiever. I began to embrace the idea of addiction and made decision to follow in the footsteps of all my literary heroes. I stepped further into the dark. I managed to continue to do well in school but without the zeal and enthusiasm of prior. I graduated high school with a 4.2 GPA which is probably the same as it would have been if I hadn't started using, the only sign that I was spiraling out of control was the blood stains from my nose as they dripped onto my finals.

I moved to San Francisco to continue my schooling. My cocaine use continued throughout, and there were boys all along the way (my other addiction). I ended up in a long term relationship but was unable to remain faithful because my drug use always came first. I began hurting my roommates with my choices but all and all I was still under the impression that my life was good and I was just doing the things that everyone does. I began burning bridges, usually around sex and drugs. I cheated on my boyfriend and got pregnant. I ran home to Southern California and had an abortion, unbeknownst to him. The day I had my abortion was another step further into the darkness. They had put me under, I was alone. There hadn't been any conversation about me keeping the baby by anyone. It was what it was. As I went under I began to have regret. When I came to, I sprang up from the hard metal slab of a bed screaming at the top of my lungs. This was the day I started using heroin, and I didn't put it down for 7 years. The light continued to dim.

My heroin and cocaine use continued and took me all over the country. I dropped out of college, and continued to rationalize my use as a sort of social experiment. Because that was what I chose to believe, and today I can say that there may have been some truth to that, as there were so many gifts of insight that I received along the way, but I fell deeper and deeper. I ended up mixed up with the cartel for a bit, murder all around me, an innocent little college girl from the suburbs. I began shooting heroin and cocaine together at an alarming rate. I was hospitalized several times due to infections in my blood. I used drugs while hospitalized, and I was in love with heroin, cocaine and a man. This man was involved with horrible things. Behind his mask of crime, furry and hate there was a glowing light. He did good things. I witnessed the struggle in him, the duality - I saw the little boy, and I loved him.

The world said he was evil, I say he was lost. When he went to prison, I fell deeper into the dark. I was obsessed with heroin, and my life was consumed with no other priorities. I remember, I would shoot up and immediately begin preparing the next shot. I started smoking crack as I had wasted all my veins. I couldn't stop - but I tried.

When the "man" went to prison, my family stepped in and tried to save me. They threw money at my problem but didn't really want to know about it. I went in and out of rehabs for the next 6 months. I had so much grief but wasn't willing to face it. I had all of these people trying to tell me I could have a happy normal life. God was knocking, but I was too angry and saddened to hear. I hated everyone, I hated myself. All I could see in anyone was darkness. There was no light in the world. People would try and put on a face of light but I could see underneath their masks only to find sadness, ego, greed, resentment, lust, dishonesty, and pride. This belief became solidified when I went into a sober living home owned by a man reputable in my community for doing good works. While I was there, I relapsed. He found out, and instead of kicking me out he told me I could stay if I agreed to have sex with him. So I did. Then I robbed him. Then I left. This was the day I began selling my body, as life had shown me this was all I had of value to anyone, not my mind, not my spirit, not anything but my flesh.

I spent the next year or so prostituting myself, walking up and down the blade. I was good at it. Not because of the sex, anyone can have sex, but because of my ability to see. I could get a man to give me everything he had just to hold him and let him cry. I was a comfort, I made people feel safe and I exploited it. I spent the next 2 years fully in the dark. As I stated earlier though, this is where I began to really meet some of the most beautiful souls I have ever encountered in my entire life – addicts lost and unwilling to return home. There was Nelo, and Blue eyes, Mama, Darling, Cloud, Disc, Pea, D, Shim, Gero, Blanc and on and on and on……beautiful, forgotten, stuck in the dark, yet filled with so much light. This became a truly dark place for me, and I couldn't get out. There where so many others with gifts of light trapped in the dark there with me - trapped by addiction.

I walked and I walked and I walked through this hell. As I stated, I was robbed, I was raped, I was beaten, I was jailed, I was cursed, I was living in a brothel but I couldn't leave, the drugs, the darkness, the sadness had such a hold on me. I ended up taking a small step back into the light when I became pregnant with my son, but my addiction had such a hold on me that I couldn't stop using. My Higher Power started showing his face more clearly, but I still couldn't turn myself all the way toward the light. When I was 6 months pregnant, my use had slowed, but not stopped, I tried but couldn't stay clean more the 3 days. My son's father had beaten me…, he was trapped in the darkest hell. For the first time in my life I truly wanted something more. I prayed out to God, tears running down my face, "PLEASE GOD!!! SEND ME TO NEW HOUSE!!!! (a local treatment center) Within a week I was arrested. I spent a month in jail before they sent me to New House. I was able to give birth to my son clean. God had answered my prayers.

But the darkness wasn't willing to give up on me quite yet. I exited treatment with my beautiful baby boy, still virtually homeless, still with an abusive boyfriend who was using heroin. Within a month I was back at it, but now I was breastfeeding. I did this for a year. It is my greatest shame - the true depths of the darkness of this disease. In spite of whatever light that was buried underneath, the darkness had won.

My son's father struggled with the darkness as much as me, but there was light in him as well. He tried to teach me about God but I was unreceptive due to the darkness and hypocrisy I saw crawling on him. I know now that the two are not mutually exclusive, that darkness and light are present in all of us all the time, and that's ok. It's just a matter of what we feed that grows stronger. I have learned through my addiction to love people in spite of their darkest moments, for they are only moments, sometimes moments spread across lifetimes.

I thank God for the darkness now. It became the catalyst for moving back into the light and reconnecting my heart to my mind. My darkest moment occurred over a period of 3 weeks. My boyfriend had come home after running off and gambling away my rent. We had made a commitment to get clean and were supposed to go to the methadone clinic that day. Instead, filled with rage, he shattered the window to get into the house. I don't know why he was so angry, except that God must have intended for it to go that way. My son sustained a cut across his forehead from the glass strewn across the apartment floor. I begged and pleaded him to take our son to the hospital but he wouldn't allow it because he knew they would remove him from our custody. I didn't care. He then began hitting and punching me. He blackened my eyes and knocked out my teeth. All the while I cowered with our son clenched close to my chest, blood still running down his face. I saw my parent's history about to repeat itself. I saw a dead child and I ran out the door, screaming and pleading to God to save him.

I begged my neighbors to call the police. Of course they didn't want to - you don't do that! I didn't care, "CALL THE POLICE!!!!!" Someone finally did, and the police arrived. He was arrested, and they ripped my handsome little boy from my arms, also addicted, due to my choices. I went to the hospital to see my son - I was numb. I wasn't going to be able to take him home, nor should I have been allowed to. I went down to the parking lot of the hospital and I cried and I cried and I cried.....but not one tear for my son. I cried because I knew I was never going to be able to use again. It was pitch black. I was fully in the dark.

I didn't get clean that day. I had to walk, and start preparing. I went to the city and spent the last 2 weeks of my addiction on skid row. I stood in front of the mirror and tried to rip off my face. The light was completely gone, but I began to pray. I prayed and I prayed and I prayed. God showed up.

I found myself walking the same streets but it wasn't like it was before. I didn't feel safe in the dark like I had for so long. I was standing at the same corner, about to do the same thing I had done countless times before, when my phone rang. It was a treatment center, "Could I please come in the following day?" Praise God!!! But my addiction still had a hold of me. I went around and gathered as many pills as I could find. I had a stash ready to carry me - I was ready for treatment, but God had a different plan. They magically disappeared from my bag. I am sure there was a logical explanation for this but I didn't know what it was, so I chose to blame God. I went to treatment.

My clean date is May 19th, 2012. It wasn't an easy path - I had to hold on with all my might. I wasn't fully convinced that I had taken the right path, but I just kept taking the next indicated step. With each step I took, God took a step closer. I wasn't fully accepting of the idea of "God" but my experience began to show me that if I walked in a bit of faith everything fell right into place, almost too perfectly. In order to get closer to God, I chose to focus on the spiritual principles laid out by the 12 Steps of NA, beginning with the concept of WE. I started with getting <u>Honest</u> and finding <u>Acceptance</u> (Step 1), This <u>Acceptance</u> has grown with time. One of my Mantras became *"It is what it is, and it's not what it's not, everyone is doing the best they can, with what they got."*

Today, my Mantras and Meditations keep me grounded and connected to my Higher Power all throughout the day.

Through my Acceptance, I have found Hope (Step 2). Through my Hope being fulfilled, I have been able to develop Faith (Step 3), which has given me Courage (Step 4) to act with Integrity (Step 5), which has made me Willing (Step 6) to practice Humility (Step 7). My Humility has allowed me to Love my brother and have Mercy (Step 8), which I do through Sound Judgment and Self-discipline (Step 9). Self-discipline has created Perseverance which has forced me to be Open-Minded (Step 10). My Open-mindedness has brought me Awareness (Step 11). That Awareness has allowed me to find ways to be of Service and ultimately foster Love (Step 12), and through this journey of Spirit I have finally been able to find a God of My Understanding. I have remembered my forgotten childhood "secret" - it is characterized by one last short story.

I had around 3 years clean and was meeting with a young woman who was new to the idea of recovery. She was lost in the dark. She shared with me her experience and inability to see any light in the world, all she saw was darkness. It was killing her and she didn't want to try. I began to tell her about my journey into the light and about God and about the good in the world. I told her that everything was exactly as it should be in that moment and that I had learned to forgive everyone everything. Gears started turning in her head and she jumped on board. She was excited and had found a sliver of hope. As we walked out of the building a woman walked by. She was disheveled and dirty, broken, and obviously tormented by addiction. The young woman I had been speaking with looked at me sadly, defeated, and said, "You say all of this and then we walk outside and this is what we see?" I turned to her and from the deepest part of my soul I said one of the truest statements I have ever felt, "What are you talking about? That woman is beautiful". That familiar smile from my childhood crept back across my face and tears filled the corners of my eyes. In that moment I knew I had finally remembered the secret that had so long ago been forgotten. I knew that my struggles with addiction were the greatest Gift I could ever ask for. Now I can see things clearly - the Dark and the Light, and all the Shadows in between. Also, I have my son back, and he knows all about God. ☺

Chapter 11

7th Chakra (Higher Power)

Location: crown of head

Responsible for the Health of: every part of the body, mind, and spirit

Represents our UNIVERSAL LOVE: attitudes, values, ethics, humanitarianism, selflessness, quality of character, pure awareness

Empowered: unity with a power greater than self, able to see joy and suffering as both having meaning and purpose, humanitarian, insight into a "vast bigger picture", ability to live in "present time"

Weakened: disconnected from source, loss of belief in a Higher Power, places conditions on "God", rejects guidance, cannot accept or understand duality, bitterness, resentfulness, self-willed, cannot love self, loss of meaning and purpose, addiction to drugs and/or alcohol

Challenge: **ALONENESS** (The key factor in the development of symptoms is the **strength** of the aloneness)

Connecting with our **Crown Chakra** comes after our enchantment with alcohol and/or drugs, and things of the material world have sufficiently waned.

Through **lack of connection**, **purpose**, and **meaning** we have suffered greatly.

For addicts and alcoholics, this experience comes earlier rather than later due to childhood histories of chaos and disappointment, and the **CONSEQUENCES** of our own **ADDICTIVE BEHAVIORS**.

By fighting the **Dark Energies** that want to claim our allegiance, as well our own **DENIAL**, we have realized that drugs, alcohol, sex, food, power, positions or possessions will not, and cannot heal our **HEART** and **SOUL**.

We have also realized that:

A **Power Greater than Ourselves** is in charge, and has
our **highest good** in mind, if only we will get out of the way.

WE understand that we haven't the ability to
determine what our "**highest good**" is.

Through what has seemed to be the most difficult, confusing, hopeless
and heartbreaking experiences, we continue to "come up for air."

The sun is still shining, the night sky is full of stars,
babies are born, and people still die.
And we are still here.

We live – God winks!
We love – God winks!
We give – God winks!
We forgive – God winks!
We fall – God winks!
We die – God winks!
We rise- God winks!

Gifts continue to arrive and obliterate our past failings,
and we pass them along…

THE GIFT OF ADDICTION HAS SAVED ME 

"No questions,
No complaints,
At Your service"

E.R.'s Story

I was born on December 23, 1953, and adopted at one or two days old. My father was Czechoslovakian and my mother Irish Catholic. I have an older sister, by about 2 ½ years, and also adopted. We have had a very complex relationship but are family. She took very good care of me for a long time…, I love my sister. I was blond haired, blue eyed and at one period that I don't remember, slim but a chunky kid. I always felt like there was something wrong with me. My parents told me at an early age that I was adopted but that was all. I know nothing about my family of origin but I would bet there's alcoholism and/ or drug addiction. My sister later in life said that they had told her that I came from a large family that couldn't keep me. I know without a shadow of doubt that my adopted family loved me…, my mother with all of her heart. She was a very kind, intelligent, creative, loving woman who had the magic of life. My relationship with my father was different. I was a very sensitive kid and cried easily. My father was first generation Czech and a military man. He was an alcoholic, and work was his primary purpose in life. He was very dedicated to his work and a good provider, but emotionally unavailable. I didn't fit, what I believe, was the kind of son my father wanted. We were never close. I don't know why they couldn't have kids. Our family had many secrets. All I ever really wanted was to be accepted by him. I cried very easily and that would make him angry. Shame messages and disapproval wound your soul. My mother tried to protect me the best she could but that just drove my father and I farther apart.

The gut-wrenching fear started at around 5-6 years old and stayed with me up until my life changed on March 9, 1987. I would lie in bed immobilized, terrified of the Werewolf and Monsters in the closet and under the bed. I would get "…, there's nothing to be afraid of", well, easy for you to say. I was OK in school, but started misbehaving to get attention. I was an OK athlete, but didn't excel at anything. I was the star pitcher for 2 years in little league and swam on the swim team but nothing was ever good enough for my father to notice. I started playing the piano at age 7-8 and found something I was good at and enjoyed. Raised Catholic, I believed in God but later in life I found that wasn't where I found connection. I was touched very deeply by music and through it connected to the magic, power of life, and the universe. I would lie outside at night and look at the Milky Way for hours. I would feel powerful when I played the piano. I was always searching for some kind of something that would just make me strong, loveable, powerful, not afraid, and somebody who people would like. I was a chunky kid and always got called names, and picked last on the teams. It was a very confusing childhood with a lot of mixed messages. I always felt so alone, and there was nothing that would take that away. When girls started to notice and like me, there was a temporary reprieve from all the feelings, and I momentarily believed that there must be something OK about me. But when it ended there I was all alone - me- very small, with no significance.

I started misbehaving around age 10, and also started smoking cigarettes. Cool kids smoked. I had also started to drink occasionally, but just experimental like kids do. It wasn't until age 15 when the magic happened. I had turned into a cool teenager by misbehaving and getting into trouble, and the girls and cool kids started to notice me. My sister had already started using drugs and I followed along. I started smoking "weed", drinking, and then started IV "Reds and "Whites". My first time "fixing" prescription opiates – "new blue morphine" the magic happened. It altered the perception of myself, and life for 18 years. It made me a tough guy-badass and took away the fear, loneliness, the belief that I was unlovable, and that there was something innately defective with me. It allowed me to do things against the values and beliefs that I was raised with. I was a different person..., finally OK. That was the beginning of the end. I threw myself into getting loaded every day, and being a tail-end hippie generation guy we did everything. We did weed, speed, heroin, all hallucinogens, reds, yellows, rainbows, and anything you could smoke drink, snort or put in a syringe, we did it. Man, I felt invincible, important, I fit in. Being recognized by the "druggies" as a cool guy took precedence over everything. I was my own man, but unfortunately my sister's negative behaviors, combined with my chaos, defiance, and self-centeredness resulted in extreme anger and rage between my father and I, which ultimately destroyed our family.

One Sunday morning after sneaking out the night before, we couldn't find mom. My friend started looking around and found her in the garage with the car running. He came running in and told my father, sister and me. We went running out and discovered that she had killed herself. She had been reading a book waiting to die - there was a note but I don't know what it said. The paramedics came and my father tried to help her, but she was dead. Coming out of the garage with rage in his eyes, my Father looked right at me and said, "You killed your mother!" I know now that he had no other way to attend to his immense heartbreaking sorrow. My father loved my mother. My mother was a staunch Catholic and practiced her belief even though she chose suicide. I know that the pain of life at that time was greater for her than any fear she may have had concerning her belief and faith. I believe my mother is in heaven today, wherever may be. My father and I had a brief chance to connect, but I chose to go live with my sister and left him all alone.

For the next 17 years, staying under the influence of something became the primary purpose in life, although that was not a conscious decision. It was just what I did. We were living in hotels robbing houses, and around Christmastime we hit this rich neighborhood. All the houses had stuff, but one house was bare. There were only presents under a Christmas tree. We stole the presents and they were all kid's toys. I was initially angry because they wouldn't pay for much dope. But later it hit me, very, very, very hard. I was raised with good values and that was just terrible thing to do, so I made a decision that drugs were bad and that I would just drink, and drink I did. This resulted in seven DUI's, and many failed relationships - a couple with women I loved very much. I did have successful jobs however; apprentice pressman, journeyman pressman, print shop manager, tree trimmer, landscaper, and gardener. But I ultimately traded those in for my alcohol addiction.

On a positive note, the harmonica playing I started at age 16 turned into a professional career. I loved the stage, the "atta boys", the women, the alcohol, and now the cocaine. But after the show, the sex and partying, I was again left alone with me, ME. The black loneliness, deep heart wrenching sadness, desperation for relief, lost- so -lost fear and rage that consumes your soul was what I was left with. I had sucked dry every friend, my sister, acquaintances, anybody I could get anything from. In November of 1986 on my 33rd birthday after my seventh DUI, I was sitting in my jail cell in disbelief, wondering how all this happened ..., but still could not stop drinking when I got out. My sister took me in, and I promised her that I wouldn't drink but didn't keep that promise. She finally kicked me out, so I went to live with the only person that would temporarily take me in. I even went to my Drunk Driving program two times drunk..., but they gave me one more chance.

I remember the day I had my moment of clarity. I knew that something had to change. I knew I was at the end. There was nothing left. I tried that Thursday morning with all the will power I could muster not to drink, but I just had to drink. I was powerless to stop. My hopelessness and desperation on that Monday, March 9, 1987, resulted in my decision to go into treatment..., a decision that changed my life forever. My sobriety date is March 10, 1987, and I have not had a drink since. My journey into recovery has been something that words can't describe. I remember when I first saw the First Step of AA - *We admitted we were powerless over alcohol and our lives were unmanageable*", my thought was that somebody finally understands!! Those first days in treatment were kind of a blur. There were people there who actually wanted to be there! I struggled with the Higher Power business because I was very mad at God for what He had done to me. When I heard you have to have a Higher Power, conscious contact, prayer, and all the rest of that STUFF, man I knew I was doomed. There were a couple of things that did make sense to me though. The Big Book says, (don't ever quote me because I internalize things the way they stick) "if we go deep within ourselves, we will find the great reality, that we believe our problems are of our own making, that the obsession will be automatically relieved without any thought or effort on our part as long as we remain spiritually fit." I was taken through all 12 Steps in my first 60 days of sobriety, which I believe is one of the primary reasons I'm still sober. The facility even hired me at 46 days sober. After I accepted the job I went out on the back porch and was gripped with that gut wrenching fear, "What have I just done? I can't stay sober! I have to drink!" At that moment I was overwhelmed with the thought that my old life, as I knew it, was over.

My new life had started. I worked at the facility, started going to college, kept working in the field of addiction, which I am still privileged and honored to be doing. I have had tremendous guides in my life, and especially in my sobriety. My father instilled in me many good ethics, hard work, perseverance, and being a man of my word. I traded in alcohol and drugs for dignity and respect which I had none of, nor did I believe I deserved. My sponsor Pete, who I love with all of my heart, showed me how powerful kindness, being of service and unconditional love can be. My kids and wives loved him, and he loved them. There are so many more wonderful amazing people that have guided and shaped me into the man I am today.

The Big Book of Alcoholics Anonymous says, "*We have gone no farther than deep within ourselves to find the great reality.*" So my journey has been on the "inside". At three years sober all my sadness surfaced because my anger had dissipated. I had been praying and had incorporated the 12 Steps into my daily life, but I needed guides to help me find emotional and spiritual sobriety. It was truly the most difficult but incredible journey. I embraced my sadness, my mother's suicide, the death and loss of what my father and I both had wanted, but didn't know how to get, my intolerance and brutality towards myself for all the destruction and hurt that I had caused the people I loved, and other blameless people. It was my time to really let go and let God and others help me heal. Talk about courage and faith! I changed! I found a way to live and attend to myself, others, and my feelings and emotions with the dignity and respect they deserve. I am now touched deeply by many things and the tears flow freely. I am a free man at last. God has done for me what I couldn't do for myself. Has given me a life I absolutely couldn't have created myself. The course of the disease has changed my wife/soulmate, our children and their children. I love my wife, our children, true friends, and the opportunity that God has given me to be a part of people's journey in sobriety and recovery. I have been given the riches of the soul - the Gifts of Addiction.

The Chakras - A Guided Meditation

Although Guided Imagery should be done with your eyes closed, just read the following exercise instead, using your imagination and intuition. While reading, be sure to align your chakras by sitting with your spine straight and your chin parallel to the floor. Try to eliminate all physical and mental distractions.

Your **Root Chakra** is located in the region at the base of your spine. The color associated with this chakra is red. Bring your awareness to this region of your body and imagine a red spinning ball of energy here. This chakra is responsible for the functioning of your immune system, skeletal system, bladder, lower back and lower extremities. Do you have any physical problems in these areas? These problems will improve as the energy from this chakra gets stronger. This is the location where we hold on to FEAR. Fear of being alone, abandoned, lost, abused, neglected, or misunderstood. This energy center is associated with your foundation, stability and security, and directly connected to your family of origin… your "tribe". You emerged from that tribe with certain feelings and beliefs about yourself. You have carried this "identity" with you all of your life. Allow yourself to acknowledge these fears, their origin, and their power. Understand that continuing to allow any dark, destructive "fear energy" to circulate within your body, mind and spirit will prevent your healing, and will only cause further pain, sorrow, and destruction. Imagine replacing these fears with faith and trust…. knowing that you are immortal and eternal….knowing that your lessons (challenges) in the classroom of this life were scripted perfectly…. knowing that you are safe here on earth as who you are, with your particular circumstances. You are supposed to be here. You were supposed to come.

Now close your eyes and let this settle into your being …

Now moving up…

Your **Second Chakra** is the sacral chakra…located along the spine at the level of the navel. The color associated with this chakra is orange. Bring your awareness to this region of your body and imagine an orange spinning ball of energy here. This chakra is responsible for the functioning of your sacral area, sacral spine, hips, reproductive system and kidneys. Do you have any physical problems in these areas? These problems will improve as the energy from this chakra gets stronger. Notice any feelings of GUILT, WORRY or ANGER here...any urge to control, or need manipulate others.... any fear of not feeling "good enough." This energy center responds to the quality of our relationships. Are we able to be flexible, nurturing, yet maintain healthy boundaries in our relationships? Or do we have a habit of controlling others or being controlled by others? Imagine the ability to set healthy boundaries, take risks, and recover from disappointments or failures. Notice the feeling in this area when you recall any "unfinished business" or resentments you still carry, or any secrets you are holding on to... Imagine letting go of all of this... Know and trust that you have been uniquely created... and are divinely nurtured, guarded and protected. You are perfect...your path is perfect... your learning is perfect. Acknowledge this. Understand that dysfunction in the 1st and 2nd chakras account for the greatest dis-ease in your body-mind-spirit.

Now close your eyes and let this settle into your being ...

Now moving up...

Your **Third Chakra** is located in the center of your torso, in the region of your solar plexus. The color associated with the third Chakra is yellow. Bring your awareness to this region of your body and imagine a yellow spinning ball of energy here. This chakra is responsible for the functioning of your pancreas, muscular system, skin, stomach and liver. Do you have any physical problems in these areas? These problems will improve as the energy from this chakra gets stronger. Notice any feelings of INFERIORITY here... or dependency on others for your identity, success or happiness. The energy from this chakra governs your personal power and strength of purpose. Notice the sensation in this area when you are feeling powerless or need approval from others. Acknowledge that it is a feeling of not being good enough, strong enough, or capable enough... Permit yourself to release these feelings and acknowledge your own personal dignity and importance... Know that you are capable... know that your particular path is perfect. Sense a feeling of expansion, courage, and personal honor... Now combine that with your deep wisdom and sweet humility... Acknowledge your unique abilities and the times that you have had to endure certain situations with patience, courage and integrity. Know that you are powerful... and can be accountable for your life, and your spiritual growth.

Now close your eyes and let this settle into your being ...

Now moving up...

Your **Fourth Chakra** is located in the area of your Heart. This is your center of love, gratitude, and forgiveness. Bring your awareness to this region of your body and imagine a shimmering green ball of energy here. This chakra is responsible for the functioning of your heart, thymus gland, blood, circulatory system and lungs. Do you have any physical problems in these areas? These problems will improve as the energy from this chakra gets stronger. Notice any feelings of resentment or bitterness that you are carrying, or any unresolved anger or grief... or any feelings of being a victim to the behavior of another person. Know that these feeling are lodged in your 2nd Chakra, preventing your heart from opening. Permit yourself to release these feelings.... forgive and let go... Sense a true love for yourself... sense a universal love for others. Know that everyone is doing exactly what they need to be doing to learn exactly what they need to be learning, and that there is a master intelligence greater than yourself. Know that you can rely upon this intelligence to orchestrate the most beneficial outcome for all involved. Allow others to experience their own choices and their own consequences without feeling the need to rescue or judge them. Know that you can detach with love and compassion... Notice this feeling of detachment, and imagine immense expansiveness and light...Notice the feeling of great gratitude and surrender. Without judgment, notice your heart opening with love and compassion for each person's challenges and obstacles.

Now close your eyes and let this settle into your being ....

Now moving up...

Your **Fifth Chakra** is located in the area of your throat. Bring your awareness to this region of your body and imagine a blue spinning ball of energy here. This chakra is responsible for the functioning of your throat, neck, thyroid gland, and upper extremities. Do you have any physical problems in these areas? These problems will improve as the energy from this chakra gets stronger. This energy center is also responsible for the quality of your choices, self-expression, honesty and creativity. When this chakra is "leaking energy" you cannot speak your own truth or define your own needs. You find that you can become co-dependent, inauthentic and lacking in the confidence and authority to make sound decisions. Know that these fears are lodged in your 1st Chakra. Allow yourself to release the need to make choices based on past false beliefs, fears, failures or insecurities. Know that your communication can be open and honest... know that you can courageously and comfortably express your own truth... realize that truth cannot be based on fear. Know that the choices you make can be based on both the wisdom of your head...and the intuition of your heart. Sense a great release...sense peace in this chakra.

Know that you are intelligent, authentic, and capable of a unique voice. Also know that you can learn and grow by taking risks.

Now close your eyes and let this settle into your being ...

Now moving up...

Your **Sixth Chakra** is located at the point between the eyebrows. It is sometimes referred to as the Spiritual Eye. It is the seat of your intuitive knowing... the seat of your wisdom. This chakra is responsible for the functioning of your brain and mind. Do you have any issues in these areas? Bring your awareness to this area by allowing your eyes to remain closed while gently lifting your inner gaze. Envision a deep indigo blue spinning ball of energy encircled in the brightest light. When life force is not flowing freely through this chakra, you may feel disconnected and detached from your emotions, yourself, and others. You feel lost and confused. You find yourself rationalizing or intellectualizing your feelings or the feelings of others... You may appear overly logical, rational, and closed minded. You may experience a fear of the truth, a fear of discipline, and a fear of change. You may experience a detached emotional state, keeping others on the "outside". However, when this chakra is empowered, you notice a pure sense of clarity and intuition...an alignment between your higher and lower chakras…and an alignment between your head and your heart… You understand that by stilling the mind, and connecting to the "God of your Understanding" in meditation, you are able to expand your consciousness, comprehend truth, access guidance, and trust your loving, intuitive heart.

Now close your eyes and let this settle into your being…

Now moving up…

Your **<u>Seventh Chakra</u>** is located at the crown of your head. It is referred to as the Crown Chakra. Bring your awareness to this region of your body and imagine a beautiful violet opalescent spinning ball of energy. This chakra is responsible for the functioning of your cerebral cortex and pineal gland. When energy is "leaking" from this chakra you may feel a loss of meaning in your life. You may question God… Why me? Why this? You may reject guidance and have great difficulty accepting the lessons that are meant for this lifetime. Allow yourself to release any thoughts or feelings of disconnection from your Higher Power. Observe that it is YOU who creates the distance…and it is YOU who must "reconnect."….and by doing so, develop a new clarity in understanding the profound meaning and purpose of both joy and suffering. At this deep level of awareness, you discover an authentic "knowing" of your path and your eternal nature. You understand the meaning of "surrender."

Now close your eyes and let this settle into your being …

Now that we have experienced each of the 7 chakras, very gently, and easily detach, and become the <u>observer</u> of **YOU**. As the observer, notice the connection between your **<u>consciousness</u>** and your **<u>circumstances</u>**. See the degree to which you create your own reality. See how your body, mind and spirit respond to the messages received from your thoughts, your beliefs, your faith…. and your fears. Understand how your consciousness can make you ill… and how your consciousness can make you well. Through Chakra Meditation, you can consciously become aware of any compromise in your system…where you are leaking the energy of your powerful, divine life force.

As the first three Chakras heal,

the higher Chakras open.

As this process continues,

we see that it is our love

that heals the body, mind and spirit,

and it is our love that touches God.

As our love touches God, God touches us

Chapter 12

More Recovery Offerings ☺

A.V.'s Story

Drugs, first and foremost, I am extremely grateful to be the one ending my relationship with you, rather than you putting an end to me. You have consistently been a part of my life since I was 20 years old. I remember meeting you once before, but you turned me off along with the immature boys who introduced me to you. I had meaningful relationships with friends and family and I was focused on going to college to obtain a degree in Journalism and Public Relations. I was goal-oriented and independent, with healthy boundaries.

In 2007, when life became too much to handle, the only thing I knew that could comfort me to the extent I needed, was you. I desperately wanted to change the way I felt. Not only did you promise me relief from my emotional anguish, you also promised me courage, confidence, wit and euphoria that I could never receive from anyone or anything else. That moment we were re-introduced I let you in without hesitation, letting you take my mind, my body and eventually my soul. All the stress and anxiety from my family's financial troubles no longer burdened me. The guilt, shame and embarrassment I felt from working at the nude strip club in order to help my parents turned into a dishonest hustle and an adrenaline rush. I fell deep under your spell. The more time we spent together the more I started losing sight of reality and of who I was.

Xanax, I underestimated you as a prescription medication. You hypnotized me to the point where I started seeking you to deal with the stress and pressure at the club. You made my six hour shifts fly by. I committed deceitful acts of lying and thieving to obtain money from customers who were only looking for an honest fantasy. I found out quickly that you had a lot more to offer than anxiety relief. You were my courage in pill form. But it was you who opened the floodgates to my world of chaos and destruction.

Meth, I made a promise to myself that I would never resort to IV drug use but the moment presented itself that hot summer day in that cheap, dirty motel room. You made me extroverted and talkative. You made me paranoid, spending countless hours online reading Government conspiracy theories. But as much as you brought me up, you brought me down to 89 pounds. You made my face look gaunt and you made my hip bones and the ribs around by back protrude. You made me stay up for days at a time walking around the Las Vegas Strip, and in and out of casinos like a mad woman. You took my beauty, my appetite, and my dignity.

Cocaine, we first met at an *In and Out* drive thru. Though I didn't turn to you as much, I was intrigued with your alternate routes of administration. Like meth, I enjoyed you most running through my veins. The media showcased many of my favorite childhood celebrities partying with you like rock stars but our parties always ended with regret, a bloody nose and an anxiety level so high that not even Xanax could pull me out of that hell hole. You gave me a false sense of pride, confidence and prestige.

Heroin, my love for you cannot compare to Xanax, Meth or Cocaine. It was you who swept me off my feet. It was love at first high. It was like Christmas morning for a child waiting to open presents before each time we got together - the way you seduced me with your ritual- the way your vapors hit and tickled the back of my throat. The dark trails of evidence you left on the silver shiny surfaces proving our love for each other. The blanket of warmness you provided me with during the winter chill. The way you removed all of my trauma and emotional pain I bottled up inside me. The way you were always available when friends and family were not. You were my ears when I needed to express, and you were my shoulders when I needed to cry. The anticipation you gave me from the last time I felt you to the next left me with the desire to always be with you. You were my ultimate form of comfort and security. Without you I could not function. I needed you the moment I woke up. I needed you to eat and sleep and to attend family gatherings - holidays, birthdays and even funerals.

As our relationship became more intense so did my struggle for survival. Because of you I did things I never thought I was capable of doing. I became a regular at the pawn shop selling my valuable possessions and gold jewelry I stole from my mother. I shoplifted and committed other petty crimes. I gave up my body, after no longer having the patience with men to sell them only the fantasy that honest lap dancers offer. I terminated two pregnancies to keep my relationship with you. Because of you I experienced homelessness seeking shelter in public restrooms and single stall family bathrooms hoping that I would not get caught. Every dollar I shamefully made went to you. You brought me around shady people who used me for the very little I had and who mentally abused me, making me feel like a worthless object. I was completely immersed in your darkness. Toward the end of our love affair you had such a firm grasp on my soul. I spent 43 days in jail for a possession charge. However, the jail sentence was a blessing in disguise. I was forced to find God, and God was revealed to me. I gained a sense of clarity sitting in the two-man cell. Aside from getting lost in the books I read, writing was my way of coping with the consequences of being with you. It provided an outlet for me to release the anxiety in that stressful environment. After about a week, I started gaining confidence each morning waking up without any physical discomfort, and with each journal entry written. I started to find myself again. After experiencing hell on Earth I was given the chance to come out of the darkness and into the light where you do not belong. You gave me the opportunity to remember the person I am by experiencing who I am not. Checking into treatment allowed me to release and process the emotional traumas that caused me to turn to you. I learned about the Gift of Addiction and the importance of "being of service." Through my personal written assignments I rediscovered my passion for writing. I have found a new way of life without you by keeping an open mind and maintaining a conscious connection to a power greater than myself. I now utilize holistic methods such as meditation and yoga to cope with stress and anxiety. I have incorporated exercise and a nutrient rich diet into my regime to bring my body and my mind back into balance. I am blessed to have new and meaningful friendships with others in recovery and to witness the transformations and magic happening in their lives. Today, my relationship with my family is the strongest that it has ever been. I have found the love within myself that you could never give me. On this illuminated path of self-discovery I have the faith and confidence that I will never have the need, nor desire to turn to you again. Without the gift of addiction, I would have no idea who God really is, or understand my connection to Him.

M.M.'s Story

My first experience with drugs was when a friend asked me if I wanted to smoke a joint at around 12 years old. Nothing became of it, as most likely it was oregano and his older brother playing a trick on him. On my 13th birthday, I came home from school to find that my dad had left town with his "unknown to anyone mistress", who just happened to be my girlfriend's mother. Only later did I find out she was only my girlfriend so my dad and his girlfriend could spend time together without raising any suspicion with my mom or her husband. Within a few days of their departure my girlfriend also left town, she was only there as a decoy. To this day I never knew why he picked that day. I know he didn't forget what day it was, as we had my favorite breakfast as a family that morning. It was a small town where everybody knew everybody, so the abandonment, humiliation, shame, anger, and blame were overwhelming. I remember my dad's mistress's husband showing me a gun and telling me he was going to find them and motioned like he was pulling the trigger. Not a happy 13th birthday for me, but rather a very heartbreaking day. Sometime shortly after that, a bottle of Boones Farm wine landed in my hand, and suddenly the pain, confusion and heartbreak lessened by "stuffing" that all inside. We owned a fairly large mechanic shop that my mom tried and failed to maintain. She closed down the shop and turned it into a pool hall. That failed as well within a year or so, but during that time I made friends with the older 16-18 year crowd. They took me under their wings, as my mom was trying to keep a roof over our heads. So at about 14 or so my dad was gone, my mom was working, and I was basically on my own hanging out with the older crowd. That led to using whatever drugs came to town from California, and always to whatever alcohol the older crew were drinking.

At about 15 ½ my mom realized what was happening to me, and that she needed to move us out of that town and away from that group. The problem was that we moved to Southern California, which was like putting the fox in the hen house. It didn't take long for the drugs and alcohol to find its way back to me, as I was still pretty much alone while my mom continued working to keep a roof over our heads. All this time, and even throughout high school, I had a full-time job, which kept me responsible, but also provided for all the pot and alcohol I wanted. Two days after high school graduation, I moved away to a one year trade school in a different state. Now I was really on my own and could do whatever I wanted, but still working 40 hours a week, and going to school 5 hours a day. Weekends were nothing but a party, while

I continued stuffing the emotions of abandonment, humiliation, shame, anger, blame, all that crap from my childhood. After a year of trade school I graduated with the top honors, and decided to move back to California. Living in my own apartment with a career in swing, the drugs faded away but the beer and tequila shots were always not far out of reach on the weekends. I was now in my mid 20's and involved with a competition sport and that required a focus on health and fitness. This effort lasted about 25 years. It was a weekend event sport with training during the week, so the alcohol consumption was reduced to mainly Saturday and Sunday nights. I retired from that sport after I married and had children, but the extra time I had allowed me the freedom to have "cocktails" during the week, which became a daily event.

As our son entered his early teens, my wife was complaining that I always had a drink in my hand (as did my dad) and wanted me to stop, as she thought I was being a bad influence. So I stopped… drinking in front of them. Yes, I would still have beer on the weekends, and occasionally during the week, but the hard alcohol stopped… in front of them. That was the beginning of my downward spiral. This is when, after about 40 years of controlling my alcohol consumption, I no longer had control over it, it had control over me. I just couldn't stop no matter how hard I tried or prayed about it. I had lost control and things were becoming unmanageable and I knew it, but I still couldn't get any sort of control over how much alcohol I was drinking.

This is when I began praying for some relief. As a child, I always believed in God. Don't ask me why, because I don't know, but I have always believed. With my praying I would sometimes get a 3 to 4 day reprieve from my drinking, but by day 4 it was always game back on.

From the house that I have lived in for 30 years now, there is a cross on the mountain, visible from my kitchen window. Approximately 15 years ago, a raging storm sadly knocked that cross down. After it happened, I realized that not only me, but probably many others have been praying to that cross for years. Looking at that mountain without the cross was very disheartening to me. So, being a member of the church at the base of that mountain, I went to the pastor and asked him if I could replace it. It wasn't just a green light; it took about 1 ½ years of persistent determination to finally get proper approval for its replacement. God's plan must have been that other individuals needed to be involved. On my daily walks while looking at that cross, I would pray for help with my addiction, but with no real results. Was I not good or faithful enough? Did God not want me to replace the cross? Asking, praying and pleading went on for many years. In addition to my prayers in and outside of church, I would also look and pray to other crosses on surrounding mountains, but to no avail. I was on the brink of destruction and my family just wouldn't take any more of it, so I realized it was time for professional help. After many sleepless nights, crying and pleading to God, I entered a local drug and alcohol rehabilitation program.

It was during this time that I learned about the word 'surrender', and the meaning behind it. One morning looking out the window of my room into the sky over the palm trees, I told God, "I surrender not only my addiction to You, but all things to You". I also told Him that I couldn't do it on my own, and that I understood that I wasn't really in control anyway. In that instant it felt like someone was pouring warm water over me from the top my head to my toes. The weight lifted and the relief I felt was absolutely amazing. The connection I felt with God instantly started to grow and continues to this day. Knowing that He really is the one in control and everything happens for HIS reasons, not mine gives me the comfort and freedom to enjoy my life and be of service to others. Life will always have its tests, but as long as I remember to surrender them to God, the burden is so much lighter. I now understand that everything works out the way it's supposed to - everything happens for a reason, GOD'S reason, GOD'S plan, not mine. I am now gaining the gift of insight and clarity to be a support and inspiration to others. That they may receive one tiny little nugget from me to help them understand the gift of addiction, and its path toward GOD is the greatest gift I could ever receive. The gift of my INTEGRITY with GOD is the single most important thing keeping me sober today. With that comes overwhelming GRATITUDE.

P.F.'s Story

I grew up in New York City and my parents were alcoholics. This is not an excuse but fact. 'Normal' life, as I look back was not so normal. My father's drinking eventually led to his being separated from us. Feeling different began. Keeping secrets was introduced as I had to lie to my mother about where my father took us when he picked us up on Sundays.

About 12 years old I was abused by a scout leader. Lying and feeling different was my new 'normal'. I felt I couldn't tell anyone. When I entered high school, I started hanging out with my neighborhood gang and I began to feel part of something. I met a young girl and began to use drugs about the same time. I was attracted to both. I liked that drugs allowed me to be part of the gang. More importantly drugs obscured the impact my past had on my present life and that was what I needed.

I was able to graduate from high school but I was "strung out" on heroin. Although I had a job, my drug use grew, causing me to have to steal to support my habit. When I finally got arrested, I got scared enough to look for a way out of my uncontrollable life. It was the Vietnam War era and I was going to be drafted. I didn't like the thought of being shot at or blown up so the Navy looked like a great alternative. Not knowing how to swim never entered my mind. I got married after "boot camp" and because I continued to drink and use drugs whenever I was able to, my wife ultimately asked me to move out. Soon after, I discharged from the service and returned to NY and restarted my love affair with heroin. I had more feelings that needed to be quieted and heroin helped do that.

I got a job with a large tech firm but my addiction cost me that opportunity. I was homeless and 'strung out' within 6 months. I signed into a long-term (3 year) State run drug program. During that time I tried 2 maintenance programs, Cyclazozine and Methadone. They didn't work but all I needed was a perception that I was trying to stop using. I just switched the type of drugs I was using. The State's last attempt to help me was a 15-day detox at the end of 3 years. After I discharged, I overdosed the next day.

A west coast drug program (SYNANON) was taking addicts, from New York, Chicago and Detroit, into their California programs at that time. Having just overdosed, it sounded like a good alternative. I really didn't think of not using but being homeless in NY during the winter made it sound like a good alternative. I found a place where I met other addicts who had been clean longer than I had used and had used longer than I was alive. The idea that I didn't have to stay an addict was made obvious. I lived in this communal lifestyle program for almost 6 years. During this time I built my self-esteem and self-worth through hard work and helping others. I left the program after my mother died. I had tremendous guilt that I was unable to help her when she needed it. With this guilt and some insurance money she left, I was ready to run back to drugs and their numbing abilities. I ran for 18 months and then entered a program that some friends from SYNANON had started in Los Angeles, CA.

While on that last run I attempted suicide by overdose. I remember asking God "Why won't you let me die? Who is going to miss this junkie?" But, my earthly journey continued and I ended up in another treatment facility. During the 18 months I was a part of that program I learned another lesson. I had not told anyone that I had tried to commit suicide before coming there. One evening after carrying a message to a Youth Authority facility, I came home and was asked by another person "How did you get here?"

I began to share the story I had made up, and a phrase "the truth will set you free" came into my mind. I stopped and shared the truth of how I got there for the first time. Another piece was added to my character. I stayed clean for 5 years until the relationship I was in broke up and I picked up again. I was off and running. This run lasted just 4 months. I met an old friend from recovery who helped me stop using. We fell in love and got married. I became a licensed contractor and she became a drug counselor. Life led us to southern California. Eventually we moved close to my father-in-law who had cancer. He died a year later, but had left my wife some money, so we bought a house. Our relationship lasted 5 years but we separated when I found out an old friend had been seeing her. I once again reached for drugs to stop the 'pain'. That evening as I swallowed the pills, I remember that the 'last thing' I wanted to do was the 'first thing' I did; I picked up to kill the pain. I was aware of everything that was going to happen: Liquor store, bar and connection. I screamed out to a God I didn't have, "God, what do I have to do to stay clean?" I know now that the God I didn't have had let me see exactly what I was setting in motion. No lie that it was going to be different this time. I had thought that I was doing everything I could to stay clean. I later realized that what I had been doing wasn't working. I did not leave the house that evening because I had been shown exactly what the outcome was going to look like. For the first time, I was unwilling to pay the price. I stood there and cried. Once more I had no defense for the feelings from my past. All I could do was cry and not leave the house.

The next day I remembered a friend I had met through my wife's work who had been going to a relationship group. I contacted him and I went to an alcohol Outpatient Program. I attended the Men's Group and they said I had to do three AA meetings a week in order to be part of it. I thought my problem was relationships, not alcohol. I let them know how busy I was and they let me know there were meetings every day and all throughout the day. So eventually I made the meetings. I was not ready for another program so I just went to the meetings. The steps, as I read them, were not something I could or wanted to do. So, meetings were all I did. After three years of untreated addiction, resentments had me thinking homicide. I went to a meeting out of town and shared my dilemma with them. I was given some suggestions to get on my knees that evening and thank my Higher Power for another day clean. In the morning, they said to get on my knees and ask for that Power to guide my day. I was told to also pray for the man I had a problem with: "To have the same as I asked for myself."

I hadn't prayed to any God for a long time, but the poison of my resentments made me willing to try something new that night. After two weeks of praying (I actually put my shoes under my bed so I needed to be on my knees), I had a moment of clarity. As I drove up the freeway and passed a billboard I had driven by hundreds of times in the past. It read "Prayer Changes Things". That morning I knew what it meant for me. I had been willing to ask for God's help and He took the obsession to harm the other person right out of me. Then I remembered when I asked Him "Why won't you let me die?" and "What do I have to do to stay clean?" He had answered those prayers, just not when I wanted them answered. He had led me to AA and the fellowship had led me back to Him. My brain felt like a pinball machine as I made connections about my life and how He had been there all the time, just waiting for me to ask for His help. I smiled and knew He had led me to the answer to all my problems.

I continued to pray each morning and night. I got a sponsor. He showed me how the 12 Steps could work in my life. The gift of the 12 Steps (the Promises) were coming through and true in my life. I began to see the reason He didn't let me die that night in 1977. He wanted me to carry His message to those still suffering. I now attend a formal church where I honor the gifts He has given me. I work in the Recovery field where I carry a message as a Counselor. I still have to work my program to maintain the gifts I am being given and to stay open to the other reasons I am alive today.

My life is full. I have a relationship with my God and have been happily married to my wife for six years. I am able to carry a message of 'Hope' and be a friend to those seeking an answer to their addictions. For this unbelievable gift, I am entirely grateful.

S.D.'s Story

My life began with two loving parents and my brother, who was four years older than me. I have so many wonderful memories of my childhood. I was blessed to grow up in a small town with a close knit community. There were always friends to play with and social activities going on. My favorite times included block parties, 4th of July parties and parties at my grandparent's house. There was a lot of drinking going on at these functions, but it didn't bother me at all. It seemed to me that the adults were just having as much fun as us kids were.

My parents didn't drink, but my grandparents did, quite frequently. I have fond memories of my Poppa's bar in their house. It was filled with shiny bottles of liquor and very fancy glasses. When we would visit Nonna and Poppa, their first question was "what can I get you to drink"? My brother and I felt very grown up while sipping our Shirley Temple's and Roy Roger's while they would partake in "adult beverages". It all seemed so happy and fun at the time. I was extremely close to my Poppa. He was my safe place. He would laugh and play with me and be so silly with me. Over time, I noticed that the more Nonna and Poppa would drink, the happier he would become and the angrier she would become. I didn't understand the role alcohol was playing in their lives. It didn't even occur to me.

We eventually moved several states away. I was heartbroken to leave my home, my friends, my school and especially my Poppa. When I was getting settled into my new life, home and school, I got some very bad news. My mom called a family meeting to tell us that Poppa had liver cancer and it was terminal. I ran to my room and began to cry, pray and beg God to let my Poppa live. I only saw him once more. He no longer had his rosy pink cheeks or his round tummy. He looked like a living skeleton to me, and it frightened me. Not long after, he died. My heart broke in a million pieces. He was my first loss to the disease of alcohol.

Around the time I was finishing middle school, my little sister was in elementary school and my brother was in high school. I was beginning to notice my brother's behavior changing. He was becoming distant, angry and depressed. He was my first best friend, but now I could feel him pulling away from me. I didn't like that feeling at all. I tried to stay connected but he would just retreat from me. It wasn't long before my brother started getting himself in trouble with our parents. He began lying frequently and being unusually secretive. He also began drinking and using drugs.

I could not understand why he was acting so reckless and not being concerned with the consequences of his behavior. I began to feel very uncomfortable with this new version of him. I loved him and didn't want anything bad to happen to him, so I began covering for him. I would keep secrets for him from my parents. I wouldn't tell them that he was drinking and smoking pot in his room. Sometimes, I would actually take the blame for him and suffer consequences for things I did not do. I used to let him hide his beer and cigarettes in my room. One time, my mom found them. I did not tell her they weren't mine, and accepted the consequences even though I had never had a sip of alcohol or smoked a cigarette in my life. I felt that I was stronger than my brother and that I could handle the punishment better than he could. I wanted to save him. He allowed it and watched while I was getting in so much trouble, knowing he was guilty….not me. I didn't want arguing and fighting in my house. I also wanted to protect my little sister from the chaos, as she was seven years younger than me and eleven years younger than my brother. I continued to enable and cover for him. I also learned that if I acted out, my parents would focus more on me and less on my brother. I was in trouble ALL of the time. I continued asking myself the same questions: Why won't he just stop? How hard can it be? Why is he ruining his life? What is wrong with him?

My brother eventually moved out of the house and out of our lives. We would get together once in a while to catch up and I even drank with him several times. That was when I realized that I could stop when I got a fuzzy buzz, but he could not. He drank and drank and drank until he could barely function. This made me wonder, was he an alcoholic? Over the years, we all got married and had our own families. He became more and more distant. On my 42nd birthday, he texted me and wished me a great day. We said "I love you". Less than two months later, he took his life. I will never be the person I was before he died. A part of me is dead too. He was my second loss to alcoholism.

Alcoholism found its way into my life again. This time, it took hold of one of my precious children. I found myself in such a dark place that I honestly thought I was going insane. I continually asked myself: What did I do wrong as a mother? How could I have prevented this disease from infecting my child? How can I fix this? Will my child die too? Thankfully, I found ALANON, a 12 Step anonymous program for anyone who is negatively affected by someone else's drinking. Within the rooms of ALANON, I found people I could relate to. These people have been right where I am. Their stories gave me hope. They were not insane anymore. They focused on themselves. They were working the steps and were regaining their joy. I thought.... I want that!

At my first meeting, I cried my eyes out. Each person who shared, reminded me of a part of myself. I slowly began reading the literature and started working the steps. I am dealing with my own character flaws, looking at my part in the chaos, and taking responsibility for my own happiness. I no longer try to control, judge, counsel, or save the alcoholics in my life. I've come to realize that I didn't cause their disease, I cannot control their disease and I cannot cure their disease. I am powerless over anyone but myself. I allow the people in my life the dignity to forge their path while I forge mine. I believe there are no mistakes, only chances to learn. I believe we are all right where we are meant to be. I have found gratitude with a capital G! My life is good. I have a beautiful, loving, close family; a husband who loves me and supports me just the way I am. My children are safe and alive. I am alive! And most importantly, I now know there is a GOD. A God who made me, and knows me, and is aware of every thought, feeling and emotion I have, or have ever had – a God who knows my beginning and my end – a God who is my heart and soul.

B.F.'s Story

Today I'm a productive member of society with a home, a family and a rewarding career that helps others see their true potential, but it wasn't always this way. Between the years of 17 to 21, I found myself homeless, wandering the streets with an obsession of the mind that blinded me to the effects of the drug that was destroying my life and killing me, Methamphetamine. I was in and out of jails and institutions, with a stigma that I thought would haunt me for an eternity with judging eyes. The last time I was in jail, however, something profound happened that I could not explain until now.

I was arrested for being under the influence of a controlled substance, and ultimately thought I was taking my last breath. I had been without food for fourteen days and without sleep for twenty two days - I was hallucinating and saying random things to people passing by, while I was fighting a tree that I thought owed me money. People walking by could see that something was wrong with me, and someone chose to call the authorities. In my jail cell, I curled myself into the fetal position - in the corner, shaking. I was ninety pounds less than a healthy person my height. My skin was dry and rough. The thought came..., I may not survive this." I heard a voice say "look at this cell - this is what addiction looks like". The voice was a deputy giving a tour for a program called the Mothers Against Drunk Driving (MADD). As I looked up I saw teenagers, one by one, look at me through a small square cell window - each face looking more disgusted than the one before. I thought to myself..., this is how I will leave this world, as an example of what not to do, as an ex- communicated man with no family or community. When the faces stopped staring at me, I got up to a small sink with an aluminum mirror above it. I looked into the mirror. My face appeared much older than it actually was. My skin was sun dried with a rough leather appearance. My eyes were blank and dull without the sparkle and curiosity they once had. There were huge black circles around my eyes. My hair was disheveled and had not been washed or cut for months, and I smelled like a wet dog that had just gotten into a fight with a skunk. I did not recognize the man in the aluminum mirror. I dropped to my knees and prayed as I never prayed before. I did not pray to get out of jail, or bargain, or make promises I could not keep. I prayed this time for those teenagers not to take the path I had taken. I prayed for my young siblings not to take the path toward destruction that I had taken. Lying there praying, I truly thought that I was going to die, until I heard another deputy say, "It's time to go - you're being released."

All of the signs were clear that I needed help and couldn't do it on my own. Typically, I would usually leave jail without thinking twice about calling anyone for help, except the drug dealer. This time I called my parents and told them that I needed help and was finally ready to follow any direction they could give me. I was genuinely sick and tired of being sick and tired. My mother gave me a phone number to a rehab in a city I have never heard of before. I called the phone number and the person on the other end of the phone said that he had one bed open, but I needed to come in right away. I went straight to the facility, which looked like a single family home in a neighborhood setting. The house did not appear to resemble what I thought a rehab should look like at all, but what did I know, never having been to a rehab before? As I walked in I heard a voice say "Welcome Home" it was the Program Director. He asked me if I wanted a tour before I committed to thirty days of living there. I followed the man, shuffling my feet, with my head down. Observing through a window to what appeared to be a group room filled with men in a circle, I turned around to the Program Director and told him, "This is not for me. The men in that circle are way older than me. I will go back out to the streets and when I get older I will come back". The director of the program looked at me and said, "At 21 I was just like you, homeless and lost until I got to this place. I thought I was going to die, but this place saved me." For the first time in a long time, I actually felt like I belonged. I signed the commitment to stay at the facility, and was actually excited to start learning the things that helped the Director change his life.

I found help in that facility that I did not think was possible, and I started to learn healthy, structured living, with responsibilities. My life was no longer about simply surviving; it was about striving for a better way to live and following the guidance of my Higher Power. I trudged along a path that I still walk along today, to a happy destiny, still conquering fears and feeling the uncomfortable pain of change. People would say "You will always be a criminal, a philanderer, a homeless junkie. You cannot change". That is not true. I believe that if you listen to your Higher Power, anything is possible and you will find your true self. I am an example of that belief.

Today, my journey in recovery is about being of service to the addict/ alcoholic who still suffers. A homeless addict like me could never have dreamed that through the Gift of Addiction, I would receive such bountiful gifts, most of all, being able to know my true self through experiencing life changing events without using drugs and alcohol. I lived in a Sober Living Home for the first year of my recovery. I went to college during the night and went to 12 Step meetings during the day. I started a Young People's meeting of Alcoholics Anonymous, and found an Accountability Support Group that kept me busy during intense cravings. A fellow member in recovery told me once, "If you can stay clean for one year and don't like what recovery has to offer, your misery can be refunded at any street corner."

During the first year of sobriety, I made multiple court appearances to reduce the 13 misdemeanors that I had accumulated in my addiction. When the last judge I needed to see to get my driver's license back told me that I had to become a productive member of society, I thought I had heard it all. But at that point the journey was just getting started. I started working two jobs, moved into an apartment, and had my first daughter. I worked hard to gain a career that gave rewards that were not just monetary rewards. At around two years clean and sober I was given the unbelievable "gift" to utilize my experience to help guide adolescents with the same disease that I have. During this time, my second daughter was born with cerebral palsy. My heart was broken at the thought of what my daughter's life would be like with such a devastating disability. It was also broken because her mother started using drugs and drinking alcohol immediately after she was born. I was again tested in my recovery with courts and judges, a familiar path I was becoming accustomed to. After multiple court hearings and endless nights of taking care of a newborn with cerebral palsy and a two year old, the court granted me full legal custody of my children. To see the life my children have today and see the smiles on their faces, I would go through any test for them. Every day being sober I feel that I am breaking a vicious cycle of addiction, passed down for generations in my family.

During this time I was also experiencing physical pain that manifested in what the doctors called Stage III Soft Tissue Sarcoma. I treated this new disease I had as my first. I followed all the doctors' directions, as I did with my AA sponsor, even on days that I did not want to accept that fact that I had a disease. Throughout all this time I was never alone. I remember in my addiction being around hundreds of people and feeling utterly alone. In my recovery I have never felt alone. I have been in remission from both my disease of addiction and cancer ever since, One Day At A Time. I moved myself and my children into a house that we would eventually purchase, and then to our permanent home. I remarried and was blessed with another daughter. As amazing as a house full of females is, I rejoiced the day I found out that I would have a son. A month later my son was born…, but passed away due to complications. My heart broke into a million pieces. All I could do was to hold on to God's hand and know that this great mystery called life is managed by a loving benefactor who knows what I do not. Everybody has emotional battle scars and obstacles, but I do not have to drink or use drugs to make them go away anymore because that would make the True me go away.

These tests, and many more to come I'm sure, have made me the man I am today. I would not change a thing. I find myself looking in the mirror and seeing a new man with aspirations, hopes and dreams. Words cannot express the gratitude I have for receiving the Gift of Addiction. My identity is no longer what it used to be, as a homeless, law breaking criminal with disregard for authority and my own well-being. Today I'm a son, a brother, a father to three beautiful girls, a husband, a loyal friend, a mentor, a teacher, a cancer survivor, a home owner and a grateful recovering addict – and a productive Member of Society. ☺

C.J.'s Story

As a child, I had no concept of spirituality or surrender. My family wasn't particularly religious or spiritual and there was never a push for me to be so. My mother was raised as a Seventh day Adventist and I can remember her talking about how much she hated going to church. Strangely enough I somehow knew that there was something much bigger than myself and many years later I would come to understand that this something was God and this God would play a huge part in the orchestration of my life.

My family was consumed by addiction. Both of my parents were alcoholics, my maternal grandmother was an alcoholic and several other relatives were either alcoholics or drug addicts. I learned at an early age that people/adults could not be trusted. On many occasions I can remember my parents fighting, both physically and verbally and how afraid I was. I was the only child then and I would hide under my covers hoping that the yelling, screaming and things being broken would stop. I had no one to talk to so I carried on as if all was normal in my household. I became an expert at keeping family secrets, but had no ability to share my feelings. Little did I know that this was the beginning of my spiritual path that God had planned for me before I even took my first breath.

When I was about 7 or 8 years old, my mother finally decided that she had had enough of my father's antics. Besides being an alcoholic, my father was unfaithful and physically abusive toward my mother. So, here we go, off to New York City where I was born. I always felt awkward and experienced the sadness of not fitting in. I also didn't feel like anyone in my family and basically didn't trust anyone. Over time, and not really understanding why, my mother began drinking. Her drinking ultimately escalated to that of a "raging alcoholic".

Throughout my childhood, my mother was in and out of hospitals more times than I can remember. I felt lost and alone in the world but didn't know where to turn or how to ask for help, hence my introduction to the dark side. I distanced myself from my family and found people I thought I could relate to. This led to a life of drinking and drug use, dangerous situations, and just not caring what happened to me.

After High School, I joined the Navy to further widen the distance between me and my family. My drinking and drug use escalated even more, but for some reason I was able to maintain myself, or so I thought. "I'm not doing too bad; I haven't been arrested yet". Four years after my military service, I was accepted into the Highway Patrol. Although I was serving as a "Peace Officer", I was spiritually bankrupt, a hopeless dope fiend, and depressed to the point of wanting to end my life. It wasn't until my mother passed away, that the gates of hell opened up and completely consumed me. I had no connection to anything or anyone including God. It was a darkness unlike anything that I had ever experienced in my life. My drinking and drug use was out of control for the next 15 years. Finally, and with nowhere else to turn, I turned to God and begged for help. I felt spiritually dead and incapable of climbing out of the pit of hell. I believe that this was the day I surrendered. I had always seen myself as a fighter but now, I had no fight left. Throughout many years, God revealed things to me that changed my life. Today I understand that we are all spiritual beings here on this planet for one thing, and that is to fulfill God's plan. All of my experiences from childhood to present were needed for me to learn this. I know now that it was necessary for me to walk through the darkness in order to understand, and be part of the light. Today I can say that I'm truly blessed and grateful for my trials and tribulations with the disease of addiction. Learning how to surrender to a "power greater than myself" means I am now free to do His will, which I have finally come to understand is my will, as well. I have been blessed with a son who is the center of my life. I get to come to work every day to do the work I love, which is helping addicts and alcoholics like myself. As they say in the program, I have *"A life beyond my wildest dreams."*

When I Remember

Sometimes when the world seems too confusing,

and I am too caught up in how I think things should be,

these are some things I can remember

to help me find my peace ♥

- ♥ That God is the doer, and I am at my best as His humble servant
- ♥ That ALL my stress comes from my expectations and attachments
- ♥ To "Keep it Simple", and not complicate my life and relationships
- ♥ That I can still love those who do not understand me – as God does
- ♥ That although I do not understand this confusing life, God does
- ♥ That the Path of Addiction is difficult for a reason – there are no mistakes
- ♥ That my unique path is meant to provide significant stress for me to reach my goal

- That God has given each of us the free will to choose light over dark, divinity over evil
- That all souls are infinitely loved and cherished by God - He has no favorites
- That Forgiveness and Gratitude are my most powerful tools
- That God understands my struggles and troubles – He made this show!
- That reliving negative situations always awakens dark energy within my body, mind and spirit – the price is too high to reminisce!
- That through God's confusing labyrinth – lies is my Purification
- To fathom the vast spiritual cosmos is the greatest adventure imaginable Oh immeasurable Joy!
- The immediate cure for my emptiness, hopelessness, restlessness or discontent is always SURRENDER and GRATITUDE
- That I cannot put conditions or expectations on God – I have to learn to trust His Divine Timing
- That applying the self-discipline to "wait" is a valuable preventative medicine for bad decisions
- That in the presence of the Dark, I must fully align with the Light, again, again and again
- That at my Darkest Moments, God is sitting right next to me in the chariot of my battle
- That "tests" arrive unannounced to drive out some spiritual weakness that is standing between me and God
- That anytime I am feeling any negative emotion, I am being tested

- That meditation increases my ability to receive information, and activates my intuition
- That meditation is the practice by which I can identify truth
- That spiritual healing is easy – I just open my heart and fall into God's arms
- That Love was the project I was assigned before I was born
- That within me is the kiss of God's love on my heart

No Questions

No Complaints

At Your Service

E P I L O G U E

In Memoriam

Toby Burditt 1968 – 2014

In his suicide note, Toby wrote:

"I am a terrible alcoholic, and I don't want to hurt anyone anymore.

"I think about suicide constantly."

He jumped off the Bay Bridge in San Francisco on September 17, 2014

As addictive genes bounce around in families and through generations, they landed in the body and consciousness of my first child. He was born on my birthday, February 16, a beautiful strawberry blond, blue-eyed bundle of pure joy - the most amazing miracle I could ever imagine. As he grew into a little boy, he was loving, funny, very artistic, and always affectionate to anyone, and everyone!! He loved drawing, painting and CARS! He was a track runner and was always in contention in school track competitions. Most of all he was sensitive, empathetic, and loyal to his family. Any stray, under privileged, lost, helpless, damaged, animal or human being touched his heart. He was also wise and intuitive – older than his years.

When he was 14 -16, I noticed the light dimming – less engaged, and less approachable. Understanding this was also just a sign of puberty, I allowed certain behaviors to go unacknowledged, but was secretly worried that he was carrying that dreaded "addictive gene". As a mother, I was in DENIAL - as a chemical dependency treatment professional, I knew there was a problem. It started with alcohol, then the use of psychedelics (LSD, etc.) in high school, and then in college, he started experimenting with other drugs, which resulted in his leaving college and entering his first rehab. From that first acknowledgment on his part of being an "alcoholic", I doubt that there were many significant periods of sobriety – he was just able to "manage and hide" his drinking. He did return to school to study photography and art, and loved the creative opportunity to use photography as a medium for his innermost feelings and emotions. He ultimately married a beautiful girl, had two adorable boys, and became the Art Director for a prestigious advertising agency in San Francisco.

I believe that his love and devotion to his family was the motivating force behind each year he chose to "stay". But as the drinking got worse, so did his unwillingness to communicate, or ask for help. When he died I didn't think I could survive the pain, anguish and indescribable heartache – the nights waking up in terror, not knowing where he was - like I had lost my child at the mall, or in a crowd of people – the moments when the pain and grief were like an all-consuming, suffocating wave, I felt I would surely die too.

There are always certain unmistakable "identifiers" unique to each personality and relationship. I will end this book by sharing with you two recent "Toby" stories unique to our relationship. ❤

Little Boy In Corduroy

When Toby was an infant, he was given a beautiful heirloom cradle. I put him in it during the day so I could keep an eye on him while working around the house. When he became fussy, I would rock the cradle, and play music to soothe him back to sleep. The recording artists I listened to during those days were Joan Baez, Bob Dylan, Judy Collins, Donovan, James Taylor, Simon & Garfunkel and Dan Fogelberg - (who remembers such great music?) Interestingly, Toby would always fall asleep when I played "Little Boy in Corduroy" by Donovan. It's a very sweet song, with rather uncharacteristic lyrics – and always sent him straight to dreamland. Throughout his childhood, I would frequently play this song for him, and it always brought a smile. I guess I could say it was "our song."

Fast forward to the day after his death….we had to go to San Francisco to identify the body. The thought of this was absolutely IMPOSSIBLE for me to comprehend. I wasn't able to consider flying because it was too complicated and difficult….I told my husband that we just needed to drive (keep our feet on the ground, so to speak) because it was simpler. Before we left, my husband suggested we get something to eat. The thought of food was immediately rejected by my entire being – no food please!! Let's just get on the road. My husband immediately refused that demand,

and suggested that we "just get some spaghetti - it's easy to eat and digest, I know it will make you feel better." We can go to the "*The Old Spaghetti Factory*", you always like it there." So rather than debate the idea further, I acquiesced, "Ok, I guess so."

Being about 4:30pm, the dinner crowd had yet to arrive. We were seated in a lonely corner of a large secluded room all by ourselves. Since I didn't want to be there anyway, I was about to suggest we leave, when the waiter arrived. I asked him why we were seated so far away, and he explained, "This is my section, and you are the first to arrive." Ok, I understand.....so we ordered our spaghetti....and waited, unsure whether we wanted to talk or just cry. I felt, nauseated, shaky, and lost in my own thoughts...everything seemed intolerably surreal. Somewhere along the trail of my wandering mind, I noticed some distant music – the piped-in kind they have in restaurants. At 4:30 in the afternoon, in a chain restaurant in San Marcos, CA, they were playing "*Little Boy in Corduroy*" by Donovan.

I about had a heart attack. T O B Y !!! Where are you??? No words can explain this experience, or how I survived it. I knew Toby was present, aware, and wanting us to know it was him. I could feel him all around us, but I couldn't touch him or see him!! My heart soared into the heavens, then broke into a million pieces again, and again, and again. Was I just dreaming this? Could the pain be any more excruciating? I didn't die that day......but I feel it could have been possible.

I am reminded by all his pictures and memorabilia, of Toby's great interest in music, photography and electronics. It must have carried over. ♥

Chamomile

When he was about 4 years old", Toby and I would take long walks down the dirt path to "Dennis and Jane's cabin. Living deep into the woods at that time, along the Pend Oreille River, in the Kootenay Mountains of British Columbia, we enjoyed conversations about his imaginary friends, *"Iba, Imna, Jugie Booby, Baba Bo, and Mauva.* Many adventures happened along this path, one of them being the visitation of a bear to Dennis and Jane's cabin resulting in a mess of flour and honey, and the disappearance of their prized harmonica.

During our walks and talks, we would pick greens from the forest to complement our garden fare for dinner. The Doukhobors taught us what we could eat out of the forest, and not get sick – if the goats ate it, we could eat it. They also taught us how to pick Chamomile buds, and dry them to make a delicious tea. Chamomile tea was Toby's very favorite. He called it Camin-meal. He liked it with lots of honey.

Fast forward to about 2 ½ years after his death…, I was taking a walk in the woods of Idyllwild, CA, not far from my "little cabin in the woods" (that's another story!), when a tsunami wave of grief hit my heart like a freight train. Though I was feeling very "heavy- hearted that afternoon, I was completely unprepared for the panic attack I experienced.

Hardly able to breathe, I stood very still and tried to calm myself and regain my equilibrium. After a few minutes, I was able to catch my breath and relax a little. What a HORRIBLE experience!!! Regardless of how long it's been, my heart breaks over and over again…..will it ever stop??? Looking down to try to "ground" myself, I realized that the little yellow buds on the teeny little flowers I was looking at were Chamomile!! I was standing in a whole circle of Chamomile flowers!! I just dropped and hugged the ground.

I now have a kitchen full of Toby's dried Chamomile tea. Gifts arrive when you least expect them. ♥

Every year our family celebrates Toby's "sobriety date" by giving him an AA coin, and sharing our tears and laughter with him. It has been almost four years now, an although the grief and healing are ongoing, God continues to give us the "Gifts of Addiction", and His LOVE. And somehow, we know that Toby is ok. ♥

Namaste'

Sherry Burditt, RN, HN-BC

As the Director of Clinical Services for Hemet Valley Recovery Center & Sage Retreat (Addiction Medicine Services, Inc.) since 2008, Sherry Burditt, RN, HN-BC is a Registered Nurse whose career spans 40 years of clinical practice in Chemical Dependency, Behavioral Health and Hospital Administration. After receiving her nurse's training in Jamestown, New York, she concentrated her practice specifically in Addiction Medicine and Behavioral Health, working with adult and adolescent populations challenged with addictions, depression, schizophrenia, eating disorders, and various affective and personality disorders. Later, as a hospital administrator, she held the responsibility as Director of Nursing, Director of Clinical Services, Director of Education, and Chief Operating Officer in Mental Health / Addiction

Medicine settings. In 2000, Sherry received Board Certification in Holistic Nursing through the American Holistic Nurses' Association. In private practice she has worked individually with private clients, provided consultation services and holistic workshops to over 30 acute care hospitals, supervised and evaluated healthcare instructors, and facilitated numerous conference and seminar presentations. Her article *Holistic Therapies in the Treatment of Addictions* was published in *Journey Magazine* in 2011. Sherry and her family live in Carlsbad, CA, and as a Kriyaban, she has practiced Raja Yoga meditation since 1974.

The 12 Steps of Alcoholics Anonymous

Step 1: We admitted we were powerless over alcohol — that our lives had become unmanageable.

Step 2: Came to believe that a Power greater than ourselves could restore us to sanity.

Step 3: Made a decision to turn our will and our lives over to the care of God as we understood Him.

Step 4: Made a searching and fearless moral inventory of ourselves.

Step 5: Admitted to God, to ourselves, and to another human being the exact nature of our wrongs.

Step 6: Were entirely ready to have God remove all these defects of character.

Step 7: Humbly asked Him to remove our shortcomings.

Step 8: Made a list of all persons we had harmed, and became willing to make amends to them all.

Step 9: Made direct amends to such people wherever possible, except when to do so would injure them or others.

Step 10: Continued to take personal inventory and when we were wrong promptly admitted it.

Step 11: Sought through prayer and meditation to improve our conscious contact with God, as we understood Him, praying only for knowledge of His will for us and the power to carry that out.

Step 12: Having had a spiritual awakening as the result of these Steps, we tried to carry this message to alcoholics, and to practice these principles in all our affairs.

The 12 Promises of Alcoholics Anonymous

1. If we are painstaking about this phase of our development, we will be amazed before we are halfway through.

2. We are going to know a new freedom and a new happiness.

3. We will not regret the past nor wish to shut the door on it.

4. We will comprehend the word serenity, and we will know peace.

5. No matter how far down the scale we have gone, we will see how our experience can benefit others.

6. That feeling of uselessness and self-pity will disappear.

7. We will lose interest in selfish things and gain interest in our fellows.

8. Self-seeking will slip away.

9. Our whole attitude and outlook upon life will change.

10. Fear of people and of economic insecurity will leave us.

11. We will intuitively know how to handle situations which used to baffle us.

12. We will suddenly realize that God is doing for us what we could not do for ourselves.

G L O S S A R Y

<u>Al-Anon</u> - A "worldwide fellowship that offers a program of recovery for the families and friends of alcoholics, whether or not the alcoholic recognizes the existence of a drinking problem or seeks help.

<u>Duality</u> – Duality refers to having two parts, often with opposite meanings, like the *duality* of good and evil. Peace and war, love and hate, up and down, and black and white are examples of dualities.

<u>Denial</u> – Denial is a state in which alcoholics/ addicts deny or distort reality. They may ignore the problem, rationalize or justify their choices and/or behaviors, minimize people's concerns, or blame others for their issues. Denial is a powerful coping mechanism to delay facing the truth.

<u>Family of Origin</u> - Family of Origin refers to the significant caretakers and siblings that a person grows up with, or the first social group to which a person belongs, which is often a person's biological family or an adoptive family.

<u>"God of Our Understanding"</u> – From the 12-Steps of AA, the concept of a Higher Power expressed in terms that anybody can conceive, accept and relate to.

<u>"A Life Beyond My Wildest Dreams"</u> - This is derived from a passage known as "*The Promises*" on pages 83 and 84 of the Big Book, AA's main text, which guarantee, among other things, that we will know "a new freedom and a new happiness," that "our whole attitude and outlook upon life will change," and that we will "intuitively know how to handle situations that used to baffle us."

<u>"Power Greater than Ourselves"</u> – The second step of AA reads as follows: "Came to believe that a Power Greater than Ourselves could restore us to sanity". ... The concept of "a Power Greater than Ourselves" is often understood as our "*Higher Power*" or, the "*God of our Understanding*".

<u>The 12 Steps</u> – From the Big Book, the set of guiding principles which outline a 12-Step course of action for personal recovery from alcohol, drugs, and other addictions.

<u>The 12 Promises</u> – From the Big Book, the *"Promises"* describe what will happen when we diligently work the steps of the 12 Step program, including renewed purpose or direction in life, acceptance of self and others, selflessness, hope, faith, less fear and worry, and redemption from past actions.

BIBLIOGRAPHY

1. Myss, C. 1988, "The Creation of Health"

   New York, Three Rivers Press

2. Myss, C. 1996, "Anatomy of the Spirit"

   New York, Harmony Books

3. Swami Saradananda, 2008, "Chakra Meditation"

   London, Duncan-Baird Publishers

4. Hicks, Esther & Jerry, 2006, "The Law of Attraction"

   Carlsbad, CA, Hay House, Inc.

5. Theresa of Avila 2008, "Interior Castle" Florida, Bridge-Logos

6. Niebuhr, R. 1892 – 1971, "The Serenity Prayer"

7. Yogananda, P. 1946, "Autobiography of a Yogi" Los Angeles, California, Self Realization Fellowship

8. Wilson, B., Smith Dr. Bob, Silkworth, Dr William, 1939 "The Big Book of Alcoholics Anonymous" Alcoholics Anonymous World Services, Inc. New York, NY

Printed in the United States
By Bookmasters